Praise for **I Love It Here**

"Clint Pulver's dedication and work as the Undercover Millennial offers a one-of-a-kind perspective that will transform leadership for years to come. This is the book your employees want you to read."

DR. JOHN C. MAXWELL, author of *The 21 Irrefutable Laws of Leadership*

"You know what I hate about leadership books? That they aren't more like this one: both challenging and prescriptive. *I Love It Here* identifies the elephant in the room, explains why it exists, then provides the solutions you need to create a workplace your employees will love. If you're ready for a dose of leadership tough love, read this book."

MARK SANBORN, author of *The Fred Factor* and *You Don't Need a Title to Be a Leader*

"This is a tremendous read that's full of leadership gold! Clint Pulver's understanding of mentorship will shift the way you view leadership and change the way you gain the trust of those in your circle of influence. It will help you elevate your performance to the next level."

STEPHEN M.R. COVEY, author of *The Speed of Trust*

"Clint Pulver understands the modern workforce—he's talked with thousands of employees as the Undercover Millennial, and he knows what makes people tick and what they want from work. We should all be listening to him to better engage, inspire, and retain talent. If you want to build a loyal, passionate workforce, you will love *I Love It Here*!"

LIZ WISEMAN, author of *Multipliers* and *Rookie Smarts*

"*I Love It Here* captures a winning formula for creating a place where the best people want and have to be, delivered with actionable insights in Clint Pulver's unmistakable style. Your talent is your company's greatest strength and you should never take them for granted."

TIM SANDERS, VP customer insights, Upwork

"Clint Pulver gives an insider's peek into what your team members think, feel, and need in a way that's eye-opening and empowering. This book offers a plan to reduce attrition, elevate engagement, cultivate creativity and collaboration, and build an organization that's as good as the people in it."

DANIEL H. PINK, author of *When*, *Drive*, and *To Sell Is Human*

"*I Love It Here* is not theoretical leadership jargon—it's an actionable narrative that will revolutionize the way you lead, and is a must-read for any leader, manager, or employee who is seeking improvement in their life and in their business."

DIANNA KOKOSZKA, former CEO, Keller Williams MAPS Coaching

"Clint Pulver lights up stages with his drums, but this book is his finest work to date. He takes readers inside the minds of employees and shows what leadership looks like from the other side. *I Love It Here* is a love letter to leadership done right, and I found myself falling in love with the principles and takeaways."

JEANETTE BENNETT, CEO, Bennett Communications

"This is one of the most important reads of the next decade for businesses and organizations of all sizes. Having read hundreds of business books, I can say confidently that there is nothing else like it on the market. Clint Pulver's deep and

thorough research provides insight into a realm of company culture that has never been fully explored. *I Love It Here* is pure gold for business owners, managers, and executives, and one of those books you'll go back to over and over again."
GREG TRIMBLE, founder, Lemonade Stand

"The biggest mistake I made in building my own businesses was assuming that everyone else was exactly like me. I wish I had Clint Pulver's book back then. He has pulled together a masterpiece for people who are trying to build a culture of passionate leaders who don't just want to do a good job, but also want to have a great life. Look around: does everyone love it here? Better start reading…"
MITCH JOEL, author of *Ctrl Alt Delete* and *Six Pixels of Separation*

"Clint Pulver is an incredible speaker and author who can connect and empower individuals from all levels of an organization, regardless of age or generation. His work and the discoveries he reveals in this book have immensely improved the performance of individual leaders and teams as a whole, and will continue to have a remarkable impact for many years to come."
BOB SOUTHWORTH, former engineering director, Hewlett Packard

"The experience and content this book provides is priceless. Clint Pulver's ability to not only capture but also engage the attention and actions of multigenerational humans is phenomenal! This book will teach you how to retain your current workforce and create a culture where everyone is seen, heard, and understood. Everyone loves to feel like they are contributing, and a part of something bigger than themselves."
BRANDON SIMMONS, chair, Premier Group International

"*I Love It Here* reads like a novel but delivers an action-oriented leadership sermon. The processes and solutions in this book will elevate the reach and influence of any leader who wants to improve the way they work with others. If you think your leadership style doesn't need to change, this book is for you."

JAMES LAWRENCE, The Iron Cowboy

"The statement 'a single moment in time can change a person's life' is a priceless principle, and something I personally experienced when I first met Clint Pulver—and listening to him certainly changed my direction in life. Whether you are just starting your career or you're a seasoned leader and manager, you will truly connect and relate to the stories, research, lessons, and experiences that he generously shares in *I Love It Here.*"

JASON GRAY, learning development consultant, Early in Career Talent

I LOVE
IT HERE

I LOVE

CLINT PULVER

IT HERE

HOW GREAT LEADERS
CREATE ORGANIZATIONS
THEIR PEOPLE
NEVER WANT TO LEAVE

PAGE TWO
BOOKS

The Undercover Millennial and the phrase
"It's not about being the best *in* the world...
it's about being the best *for* the world"
are registered trademarks of CRP Enterprises.

Cataloguing in publication information is
available from Library and Archives Canada.
ISBN 978-1-989603-37-6 (paperback)
ISBN 978-1-989603-38-3 (ebook)

Page Two
pagetwo.com

Edited by Melissa Edwards
Proofread by Alison Strobel
Cover and interior design by Peter Cocking
Printed and bound in Canada by Marquis
Distributed in Canada by Raincoast Books
Distributed in the US and internationally by Macmillan

23 24 25   8 7 6

clintpulver.com

To my leading lady, Kelly. "Best of wives, and best of women." Love you always.

———————

To the mentors in my life who have connected me to my dreams. I will never forget you.

———————

To the thousands of employees who spoke their truth, and made this book possible. These are their stories.

CONTENTS

1 A Single Moment in Time *1*

2 Are You the Problem or the Solution? *19*

3 Creating Your Dream Team *37*

4 The Mentor Manager *55*

5 Sparking the Possibility *79*

6 Keep It Simple *105*

7 Give Them the Wheel and Let Them Drive *123*

8 Always Be Flying the Airplane *137*

9 Brace for Impact *155*

10 Your Personal Board of Mentors *173*

11 Helping Them Live, Not Just Exist *189*

12 Small Things over a Long Period of Time *209*

Acknowledgments *217*

Notes *219*

I had opened up
Pandora's box. With
just one question
**it all looked
suddenly different**.

— 1 —

A SINGLE MOMENT IN TIME

We do not remember days, we remember moments.

CESARE PAVESE

SINGLE MOMENT in time can change a person's life. I believe this firmly, just as I believe that it's the small and simple moments that compound over time to write our life story. Some of these moments may feel trivial, others leave monumental consequences—both good and bad—but together they are always driving us to our next destination.

It was one of these pivotal moments that led me to create a company and a movement while I was in my twenties—a decision that has allowed me to work with some of the most remarkable organizations and corporations in the world.

How the Undercover Millennial Program Came to Be

In the fall of 2015, I embarked on a five-day business trip with a group of CEOs and other executives to learn from

1

some of the best business leaders in the country. My small troop consisted of nine individuals who had very impressive experience in various industries. Being the youngest in the group, I was passionate, hungry, eager to rub shoulders with amazing leaders, and hopeful that what I learned on this trip would help me grow into someone equally as accomplished and influential.

During this experience, I had the chance to spend time with people like Brandon Steiner of Steiner Sports Memorabilia, a very successful sports marketer and businessman who capitalized on his purchase of the old Yankee Stadium and made part of his fortune by selling bottled dirt and other random Yankee paraphernalia to die-hard fans. We met with a few other business experts as well, and I was fascinated by their stories, their strategies, and the things they had done to make a living and an impact.

On the last day of our trip, we were given the opportunity to interview the CEO of a different major sporting goods enterprise. (Lots of "sports meetings" happened on this trip.) We were brought to one of his outlets, the flagship of several hundred stores in a chain that had spread across the nation. By the looks of the large, thriving space, there was no end in sight to this CEO's success.

It was absolutely beautiful. The walls were lined with the newest equipment and the racks were full of the latest trends in athletic wear from Nike, Adidas, Under Armour, and more. Everything was neatly hung and smelled of clean rubber. I'm not even the biggest sports fan, but as I walked through this palace of athleticism and saw all of the employees cheerfully helping customers, I couldn't help but think that this was a place I would have liked to have worked at when I was younger.

Eventually, our small group found its way to the back of the store, where the CEO was waiting to meet us. He was a fairly tall gentleman, likely in his late fifties. By the way he carried himself and the way he began answering our questions before we had finished asking them, it was obvious he was the one in charge. I was impressed that he would take thirty minutes out of his day to speak with us: he didn't have a clue who we were or what our backgrounds consisted of, nor did he ask.

The CEO's business philosophy was this: "You grow, or you die." This seemed fitting for a man who had survived decades of fluctuating economic hardships and shifting business trends. He briefly told us how he got involved with his company, what he loved about it, and how his retail and sales systems had morphed over the years to keep up with the rapidly changing market.

At the end of his talk, the CEO took us on a tour of his store—though simply calling it a store seems insufficient. The space was a wonderland of everything sports-related, and he was the Willy Wonka of it all. "The old brick-and-mortar mentality of doing business, where people walk into your store and buy something, is no longer the way it's done," he said, gesturing at the impressive assortment of sports gear. "It's archaic. You can't run businesses off that model anymore." He paused, turning his gaze toward us. "Seventy percent of our sales are online now. Not through the outlets, not even through the stores. That's the way it is now. It's always changing. You want to survive, you gotta keep up." He raised his hand and made a gesture of emphasis, jabbing the air to punctuate each word: "If you're not growing, you're dead."

It was intense, and these startling words seemed to give everyone pause as the CEO went on to talk about the massive shift they had to make toward online sales, what it was like being forced to work through re-sellers like Amazon, and having to run targeted ads on platforms like Instagram and Facebook.

"We do a fraction of the old-school marketing that we used to," he said. "Everything is digital now, and our ability to stay alive and successful means that we've had to create a whole new model to attract and entice our customers." He turned to face us again, arms folded and face stern. "I'll say it again: You want to survive? Then you've got to keep up. Grow or die. Any questions?"

I did have questions. As we had been wandering through the store, I was watching all of the CEO's floor staff engaging with customers, selling merchandise, and ringing in purchases, just like retail salespeople have always done. I wanted to know about how all this constant change in the retail model had affected how the business trained and managed its employees. I raised my hand, and he nodded at me.

"So," I said. "You've made all these changes to maintain the loyalty of your customers, and it seems to be working out really well. In your experience, have you noticed any differences in your employees and the way they work? Have you also had to change the way you manage employees today, versus the way you had to, say, twenty years ago?"

He didn't hesitate for a moment. "Nope," he said. "The way I managed twenty years ago is the same way I manage today. And you know what? It works! We get results." He smiled and unfolded his arms, sweeping them out to present his beautiful store and colorful merchandise. *Look at my success*, he seemed to say. *That's all the proof you need.*

This response surprised me. I might not have been in the business world for as long as he had, but the dots just didn't connect. This CEO knew he needed to constantly shift his practices to meet the ever-changing needs of the market and his customers, but when it came to his management style, he saw zero need for change.

The conversation moved on as others in the group asked questions like "What was your first job?" and "Who has had the greatest impact on your business career?" and "How old were you when you became a CEO?" But I was hardly listening. I couldn't get my mind off what he had said about managing his employees. I looked again around the store, paying closer attention to the frontline staff members who were working the floor. Many appeared to be of college age; a few seemed like they were still in high school. "Huh," I thought to myself. "All millennials, like me. Many even younger."

This was also a time when the overall perception of my generation was perhaps at its worst: many saw millennials as entitled, distracted, unwilling to spend any time in the trenches, free from the expectations and burdens carried by the generations before us.

The Generations

Baby boomers	Born 1946–1964
Gen X	Born 1965–1980
Millennials / Gen Y	Born 1981–1996
Gen Z, centennials, or zoomers	Born 1997–2012

Source: Pew Research[1]

My generation is older now, and perhaps (I like to think) we are proving our mettle. Today, a scene like the one I observed at that sports store would likely be populated by floor staff from Gen Z (also known as centennials or sometimes zoomers), with a few millennial supervisors in the mix. But I would be thinking the same thing today as I thought back then when that CEO said, "Nope. The way I managed twenty years ago is the same way I manage today. And you know what? It works! We get results."

Would his employees say the same thing? Did his management style actually work? Was he really getting the results he thought he was?

At the end of the interview's scheduled time, the CEO bellowed, "All right, I have to go. But I'll tell you what—you can have anything in the store for a discount, say... 60 percent off. That sound good? Great, get outta here." We thanked him for his time and spread out into the store to buy some new athletic apparel at a generously discounted price. But instead of looking at jerseys and running shoes, I again found myself carefully watching the employees as they worked away at hanging clothes, staffing the registers, and helping customers find the right items. They all seemed friendly enough, so when my curiosity got the better of me, I approached the nearest one. He was a younger guy, somewhere between eighteen and twenty. He had a very bright smile, which was nicely complemented by his crisp, company-branded shirt. He had a nametag on—for privacy's sake, let's say it read "Derek."

"Hey... I'm kind of curious," I said. "What's it like to work here?"

Derek looked at me. "You honestly want to know?" he asked.

"Yeah, I do. Seems like a really cool place."

Derek looked around the store cautiously, and I suddenly felt as if I had just kicked off some kind of illegal drug exchange. He pressed in a little closer, and when he was sure no one could hear us, he said, "I hate this place."

Wow. I wanted to know more. "Really?" I said. "What do you mean?"

"Well—I literally feel like a number when I'm here," answered Derek. "I clock in and out as fast as possible."

I had opened up Pandora's box. The CEO had seemed so sure, so confident in the way he managed his business, and with just one question it all looked suddenly different. For

And there it was—
the single moment
in time that **shifted
my perspective**.

several minutes, I listened as Derek told me how he couldn't stand the company or his managers, how he felt like the people in charge were inappropriately controlling and misused their authority, and how he keenly felt a lack of authentic care for him as a person—or even just as an employee. To him, the store was disorganized, with no structure or direction; it wasn't clear who was responsible for doing what or how tasks could be done more efficiently. That kind of chaos didn't inspire confidence in Derek, and opportunities for growth seemed limited.

"I've got things I want to do, ya know? I've got a lot I want to be, and there's not really a future here," he told me sadly.

"So, why are you working here?" I asked. I was legitimately curious, given his list of grievances.

"Oh, I've already applied to three other places. As soon as I get an offer, I'm gone."

As Derek said this, a customer approached needing assistance and he turned away to help them. As he guided the customer away down the aisle, I thought, "Man, either this dude is having a *really* bad day, or the reality of what's happening in this store is totally different from what the CEO believes about the culture of his organization." One opinion does not give an accurate picture, so I moved to a different area of the store and tried again. I casually walked up to another employee, and asked the same questions.

Then, I approached another employee.

And then another.

By the end of the forty-five minutes we had been given to shop, I had secretly interviewed six of this CEO's employees. I asked them all similar questions in the same general pattern. And at the end of these various conversations, five of the six employees had told me they were already looking to leave the company, or that they would be gone in three months or less.

Five out of six! Granted, I had taken a small sample in this impulsive experiment, but if more than 80 percent of your workforce—or even of a randomly chosen part of it—plans to leave, something is probably very wrong.

As I walked out of the store that day, I realized there is a major gap between what an employer perceives and what their employees expect—not just in that store on that day, but in the workplace in general—and that this problem needs to be solved. I kept thinking about the employees' responses, their needs, and the simple things they were looking for (and not finding) in their jobs. Those six employees had given me truth, insight, ideas, and perspectives that had been whooshing right over the head of their CEO, despite his considerable height.

And there it was—the single moment in time that shifted my perspective.

I kept thinking back to my early work experiences in high school, in college, and even after college. I had worked with some pretty good companies along the way (and some not-so-good ones as well). Some of those companies even tried to understand their employees through the ever-popular employee survey, a well-intentioned, homogenized fill-in-the-bubble attempt to get information from people at every level of an organization. I know this is a favorite tactic in corporate America, because I have taken several over the course of my early employment history. Companies who give these surveys to their employees often believe this practice will help them learn things about their operations, gain genuine insight into their employees' relationships with their managers, and discover ways they could improve. Of course, each time I took one of these surveys, I was assured that my answers would remain anonymous and my identity would be protected, but with little reason to believe that, I wasn't likely to be honest and risk getting fired or held back for some perceived laundry list of grievances—I had no plans to take that chance, and not many of my fellow employees did either.

Some companies I worked for took a different tactic: the one-on-one meeting with a manager. These felt no safer—my blood pressure would soar as we went over all of the progress I had made, or lack thereof, and fine-tooth-combed my performance over the past month or quarter or year. At the end of one of these meetings, my manager asked me to tell him what I didn't like about his management style, and advise him on how he could improve. How awkward! Did I like the guy? Not really. He micromanaged everything I did, and didn't practice what he preached about performance standards, work ethic, or goals. Was I about to tell him these things to his face? Absolutely not. I'm not averse to face-to-face conversation, or even to actual conflict or confrontation when needed—but many, many people are, so imagine the difficulty they'd have with telling their boss what needs to change for them to love their job.

The day I spoke with those six employees in that sporting goods store, I had a pivotal realization. I was nobody of importance to them. Their relationship to me had zero impact on their job security. I wasn't their manager, I wasn't their boss, I wasn't the owner, and I wasn't some HR person conducting a company survey. I was simply another millennial—just like them. My lack of association with their company created the ultimate safe environment for them to speak their truth about their experiences. In our brief time together, those employees were not afraid of any repercussions on their job or on how their manager might see or relate to them. And even if they did see a risk, they knew they could find another job somewhere else, in no time at all.

That's when it hit me: What if the CEO could have heard his employees' responses, stories, feelings, and ideas? Imagine how that information and insight could have helped him understand his real-world company culture—and what he'd need to change to retain his employees, and get the most from their potential.

According to the Work Institute's *2020 Retention Report*,[2] 27 percent of U.S. employees quit their jobs in the previous year. And, among those, 78 percent left for preventable reasons, such as scheduling problems, a desire for more positive relationships with management, a lack of growth opportunities, or dissatisfaction with compensation and benefits. That's a lot of people quitting because of a disconnect between what they need and what their employer is providing.

What if we could change that?

Just think about it! What if we could bridge the gap between employees and employers by having a genuine conversation with both? What if we could understand the needs and feelings of employees, then bring those needs to organizational leaders so they'd have real data to draw from? With such a bridge in understanding, both employers and employees would benefit. Using this information, employers could implement new strategies. And those strategies would actually work, because they would target the true needs of the employees. Here was the missing link that could solve the disconnect between employers and their employees—real honest answers to real honest questions.

And that's when the Undercover Millennial was born.

What Is the Undercover Millennial Program?

The Undercover Millennial program gives business owners and the leaders who work for them an inside look at how their employees are doing, and what they really need from their employment. Don't let the name fool you: millennials are not the sole focus of this program. Yes, the project started as a way to understand millennials working in retail (for the main reason that I am a millennial, and at the time most frontline employees were as well), but as that generation grew and evolved, so did we—expanding our approach and methods to glean insights from workplaces that range from offices to manufacturing facilities and more. We also still work with retail and other customer-facing businesses, but now, of course, we've again adapted our approach to relate to and communicate with Gen Z employees. And I expect we'll continue to evolve as new generations enter the workforce and bring their unique perspectives with them.

By now I have interviewed, while undercover, thousands of employees across the globe, from hundreds of organizations in various industries, like food and beverage, hospitality, education, healthcare, retail, technology, automotive, and housing and construction. And my research and support team has interviewed countless more. The data we have collected is the power behind this book, and it has come from the many employees who weren't aware that their stories were truly being heard. This anonymity has allowed us to gather and compile authentic and unbiased research to help us better understand employee retention and turnover reduction.

Our process for collecting data is simple. The organizations we partner with give us permission to go into their stores, office properties, or other branches of their franchises, posing as young adults looking for a new job. We take care to look as approachable as possible—dress like they dress; talk like peers. We simply walk into one of their stores or offices, find the first employee who is free, and ask, "Hey—I'm looking for a job and I'm thinking of applying here. I wanted to see... do you like working here?"

That's all it takes. Right out of the gate, this simple question gives people the liberty to express their thoughts about why they would or would not recommend their place of employment. The conversation quickly moves through subjects like pay grade, management style, and work environment, all at the employee's guidance. To help identify consistent trends in a company and what matters most to their employees, we include these questions in every interview:

- On a scale from 1 to 10—with 1 being "I hate it" and 10 being "I'd never want to work anywhere else"—how much do you love your job?

- *If the answer is higher than 8 or lower than 5*: What's the number one reason why?

- What's the greatest thing the company does for you that keeps you here?

Depending on the size of the organization and the scale at which the management wants us to work, we can usually interview anywhere from fifty to three hundred employees, all the while looking for emerging positive and negative trends. The employees' privacy is maintained and their identities are protected. Because different states have different rules about recording people, some interviews are filmed with undercover cameras and some are not. When interviews are filmed, employees' faces are blurred, and voices are changed if necessary. When interviews are not filmed, we collect the themes and data in a spreadsheet specific to each company. Employees' answers and experiences are compiled, studied, and evaluated, and are sometimes shown as a video compilation as part of our presentation to management to help the company better understand what's going on with

---

If you want to create lasting, meaningful change, **you have to talk about solutions**.

---

their employees—always while still protecting the privacy of the employees. Their valuable insight and honest answers then form the foundation of actionable ideas that will help the company increase engagement and loyalty.

As you read through the rest of this book, you will experience many of the encounters and personal stories I have been privileged to hear while undercover. One thing to note: for obvious reasons, I have changed the names and identifying details for most of the companies and employees you're going to read about. In the few cases where I have not given a pseudonym, the person or company gave me permission to use their name.

Why "I Love It Here"?

Amidst all of the questions and answers, the most significant moments in our research occur when an employee passionately responds, "I love it here!" This powerful declaration is always followed with incredible stories that reflect universal principles that their leaders have implemented, and simple yet consistent actions and attitudes that help people feel seen, heard, and understood. Through years of hearing these stories, we have discovered key ingredients that make a company not only successful, but significant—an organization that infuses their business with a sense of purpose and creates a culture of caring and service. We have uncovered how these great leaders use those key elements to provide an atmosphere that their employees love to work in. In essence, we found answers that every organizational leader needs to know.

This book was created from the experiences, comments, and suggestions of the employees we have met through the Undercover Millennial program. Nearly everything you are about to read—strategies, tactics, ideas—came from those employees. This information emphasizes what works in businesses and in other organizations. This is not another leadership book written by a self-proclaimed leadership expert; rather, it's the product of satisfied and fulfilled employees who knew when their leaders were getting it right.

If you want to create lasting, meaningful change, you have to talk about solutions, not just problems. This book provides solution-based principles that can help you create an organization that your people never want to leave. Your company can be a place that is more than a fancy facade. A place that has an authentic core built on valuing the individual. A place where people don't just survive, but thrive.

MASTERING YOUR MOMENTS

As you read this book, I want you to see it as more than just another manual on leadership. These pages can lead you through a transformative experience as you strive to create and learn how to design meaningful moments for yourself and for your employees. Once you learn the basic ingredients of these moments and master the creation of them, your business will take a drastic shift for the better.

This is the first of the Mastering Your Moments sections that you will find at the end of each chapter. Pay attention to these questions and challenges, and commit right now to doing them each at least once. Taking this time to reflect (and act) will help you internalize and apply everything that you read. Do it however feels right: dive in as soon as you read each chapter, do them all when you have finished the book, or even revisit specific points as you need to down the line when you want to refresh yourself on a particular strategy.

Find a system that works for you, and go for it. Be honest as you answer the questions and do the challenges—that's how you will gain the knowledge and skills you need to create meaningful moments for your employees, and find greater success and fulfillment in your personal and professional life.

Question #1: What kind of culture currently exists within your organization? Choose three adjectives that describe it.

Question #2: What kind of culture would you like to have in your organization? Now choose three adjectives to describe that. Be specific, and go into greater detail if you can.

Question #3: Review all of the adjectives you've written down from both questions, and pick the one you feel is the most important within your organization—defining "important" in whatever way feels right to you. Now take a few moments and describe *why* that word is the most important.

Challenge: Make meaningful moments

Your challenge (if you choose to accept it) is to complete this book. Answer the questions honestly, commit to doing all of the remaining challenges, and witness the results this work will have in your relationship with your employees. As you complete the Mastering Your Moments for each chapter, you will find that this book is becoming a map and guide for your leadership journey. Refer to it often, apply its principles, then watch as your business becomes a place where employees can truly say, "I love it here."

The reality is this:
if your people can't grow
where they are, **they
will leave and
grow somewhere else**.

— 2 —

ARE YOU THE PROBLEM OR THE SOLUTION?

*If you define the problem
correctly, you almost have the solution.*
STEVE JOBS

F YOU'RE reading this book, you're likely in a position of leadership. Perhaps you're a supervisor, a manager, an administrator, an educator, a CEO, or even someone aspiring to one those positions. Perhaps you're a parent who is trying to better understand the principles of connection to improve your communication with your children or partner. In any of these cases, you know very well that while leadership isn't easy, it is a vital part of maintaining and retaining relationships. So often, organizations look at their turnover rate and scratch their heads, wondering why it's so high. Here's the truth: as a leader, you're either the number one reason your people stay, or you're the number one reason they leave.

When we work with an organization to uncover why their employees are leaving, we always discover a variety of reasons, ranging from wanting better pay or a shorter commute or different hours. But behind all of those individual, surface-level needs, there is always one primary contributing factor. And that's leadership—or the lack thereof.

Employees are not quitting companies—they're quitting *bosses*. Our Undercover Millennial program has found that over 75 percent of all organizational turnover can be traced back to poor management. Among all of the interviews we have conducted with so many thousands of employees, again and again we have heard things like:

"My manager keeps changing my schedule."

"They just micromanage everything."

"I hate it when they come into the store to visit."

"I don't really know them."

"They're always mad about something."

The list goes on: too much criticism, not enough connection, inconsistency.

But it's not always bad—many times, we hear the opposite. And guess what? When we look for the contributing factors behind comments like "Man, I just love it here" or "This is the best job—I love coming to work!" the answer is exactly the same as with the negative feedback: it's about the management.

"They care about us as employees and as people."

"The company cares about my family and my quality of life outside of work."

"The company grows me as a person through professional development and learning programs."

"They help us become better co-workers, better leaders, better humans."

Companies with higher loyalty and retention rates have earned the right to keep their talent. And they have done that through the kind of leadership that increases employee engagement and satisfaction.

The Trouble with Turnover

Since implementing the Undercover Millennial program in various organizations and corporations, we have found that roughly 60 percent of the employees we interview are looking for new employment. Sixty percent! On average, over *half* of your workforce is ready to bounce the moment something better comes along.

You might think that the skyrocketing unemployment rate that attended the COVID-19 pandemic has made it a bit more challenging for employees to consider leaving, but the economy will recover and unemployment will decrease again. When that happens, a large portion of your workforce will once again be on the lookout for better opportunities. And if any company out there didn't take extreme care to look out for the well-being of their essential workers in every way they could during the pandemic, they shouldn't be surprised if those employees remember, and are no longer willing to work for them once things get back to normal.

The reality is this: if your people can't grow where they are, they will leave and grow somewhere else.

Now, you and I both know that it's nearly impossible for a company to retain 100 percent of their employees. All organizations, even the very best ones, lose employees—it's a natural part of business. People move or retire, health issues arise, schooling gets in the way, they find a better fit or decide to change career paths, and any number of other situations can come up to cause an employee to leave. You may even think your turnover rate is hardly significant. But don't be fooled: there's still information in there that you need to think about.

Some leaders see employee turnover as the equivalent of a paper cut. A paper cut doesn't seem like such a big deal, right? It stings a little and gets in the way for a moment, but if you throw a Band-Aid on it, you can usually forget it's there. But what happens when you run out of Band-Aids? Or worse, what happens if your organization is small, with ten or fifteen employees? Suddenly that little cut is more than just a flesh wound.

Consider these facts:

- Employee turnover cost U.S. companies more than $630 billion in 2019, according to the Work Institute.[1]

- The cost of turning over an entry-level employee is about 50 percent of their annual salary, according to *Forbes*.[2] For a mid-level employee, that cost is 125 percent. And for a senior executive, you are looking at a cost of 200 percent of their salary.

- Similarly, the cost of replacing supervisory, technical, and management personnel can reach from 50 to several hundred percent of the person's salary, according to the Society for Human Research Management Foundation.[3]

And the situation is only expected to get more challenging. According to the Work Institute's *2020 Retention Report*, turnover has already increased by 88 percent since 2010. And by 2023, more than one in three workers will voluntarily quit.[4]

While these projections are dire, they don't need to be your reality. Your company could be the one that not only retains employees, but even attracts great talent from the companies that aren't making the effort to ensure their people want to stay.

Before we talk about how to make your workplace one that keeps people wanting to stay, let me paint a picture of what it's like when you lose an employee. Say, for example, that you run a graphic design company or a full-service marketing firm and your head designer gives you two weeks' notice because she was offered a better job elsewhere. Here's one way this situation could play out:

Step one: The head designer hands in her notice, then stops taking on new projects that come in. Instead, she hands them off, along with some of her current projects, and starts picking away a little at clearing out her desk every day. She may not have physically left yet, but she's already checked out, and she's not focusing as well as she used to on any projects she's wrapping up.

Step two: Maybe she's feeling anxious about the exit interview—many of the employees we've met with have talked about the inherent awkwardness of these interviews, and have worried about the repercussions of answering honestly, even though they're leaving. Her anxiety over that last hurdle is causing her to lose even more focus; it also means that you aren't likely to get honest, actionable answers about what you can fix.

Step three: There will likely be a gap between when the head designer leaves and when her replacement comes on board and gets up to speed. During that time, the rest of your designers are scrambling to get all their work done. They're feeling tired and overloaded—a loss in morale that can lead to an even greater loss in productivity, and may even require proactive measures on your part to prevent anyone else from jumping ship. If they're putting in extra hours to compensate for the missing designer, that might mean overtime too, or some other kind of compensation to show your appreciation for their extra efforts.

Step four: Someone in your leadership team now has to devote time and resources to searching for the right person to fill the vacant position. If you're not promoting from within or hiring locally, you'll likely have to pay for advertising or recruitment assistance, or even travel costs to bring a potential hire in for one or more interviews. There might be a signing bonus, a referral payout, or relocation costs.

Step five: Once you do find the perfect person to fill the position, you have to spend the first several weeks on orientation and training so that they'll be familiar with the company and its clients. The new head designer may then take several more months to fully learn the position and develop a relationship with your clients to achieve the same level of competence of the previous designer.

Step six: While you look to hire or onboard the new head designer, everyone is scrambling to get their projects done. Details start falling through the cracks, along with that extra personal touch your company is known for. Less time is being given to nurturing relationships with clients—and the clients who were used to working with the departing designer may start considering their options.

Step seven: Your HR manager has to get busy pulling together the necessary paperwork and prepping for the exit interview. That all takes time. And, don't forget: as the designer leaves, all of the time and money you invested in her leaves too—that includes training and conferences she attended, skills she developed on the job, and everything she's learned about your company and your clients.

One exit, many ripple effects. If you spread out the total cost from that Work Institute study across every turnover, you could peg the price tag for replacing an employee at an average of $15,000. But there's no telling how much any given company is negatively affected beyond that price tag, all because one employee struggled to "love it here."

What will happen if you don't invest in your people? They'll leave anyway. Or, worse, they'll mentally quit, and stay.

Of course, that scenario assumes the designer gives two weeks' notice. What if an employee just walks out, with no notice and no one to fill the gap? How would that affect a retailer? Without enough cashiers, your lines could increase, causing complaints for both customers and the remaining employees. Customers could leave unhappy, deciding to shop at your competitor's store instead, while the extra physical and emotional load could cause employees to feel overworked and underpaid, leading to further losses.

Can you see how, ultimately, your employee turnover is more than just a paper cut? If it's as repetitive as it can be for many companies, it could be a potential bleed-out.

Think about your unique organization. How does employee turnover affect you? How does it affect your employees, and your bottom line? Consider this: at your organization, how much time does it take for a new employee to feel like an important, knowledgeable, and competent part of your team? Six months? A year? What are the costs for each new employee to achieve the competence of their predecessor? What kind of onboarding process do your new employees undergo, and how long does that take? How much software and how many company-specific procedures do they need to learn? How many co-workers do they need to get acquainted with to the point that they are able to collaborate?

While the designer scenario won't apply to everyone, and all of these costs I just listed are not associated with every single turnover you may experience, it's important for you to think through your hiring, training, and exit processes and pinpoint all of the ways your company is affected when someone chooses to walk away. If you don't know how turnover is affecting your organization or why people are leaving, you will continue to experience loss after loss until you diagnose the real problem—and correct it.

One more thing: the statistics and scenarios I've presented show the costs incurred when an employee leaves. But what if the unhappy employee stays? What if you made a bad hire, or the person starts out with enthusiasm but eventually loses interest or gets disillusioned? The productivity lag is certainly going to cost the company financially, but this situation can also cause an even bigger problem. If you have one employee who is consistently negative and not putting in a full effort, that attitude and behavior can spread throughout your team. Pretty soon, you're going to have a workplace with very little progress.

A Changing Workforce

If you haven't noticed that there has been a significant change in the workforce, you haven't been paying attention. We discovered quickly that millennials have a specific set of needs and aims, and by now you may have learned and adapted to that as well. But millennials are quickly becoming replaced in the front lines by the generation behind them—who will be replaced themselves, and so on and so on, decade after decade. You need to adopt a new way of relating to your employees that will help you recognize and adapt to new approaches for each generation as your workplace, and the world we live in, continuously evolves.

Unfortunately, not everyone is comfortable with accepting new ways of working. Tom Gimbel, CEO of LaSalle Network, framed it very well when he said this in *Fortune* magazine:[5]

> The conflict between younger and older generations in the workplace is due to negative assumptions. Many baby boomers see millennials as impatient, unprofessional, and lazy, while millennials may see baby boomers as unapproachable

or old-school. At the end of the day, your age has nothing to do with your success; your execution does. If that message is not conveyed from the top, these generations may clash.

And the difference goes further than ways of working—the generations can misunderstand each other on things as fundamental as values. The *2018 Deloitte Millennial Survey*[6] revealed that the younger generation often sees a "mismatch" between what they think a business should be trying to achieve and the actual priorities they see playing out the workplace. "Companies and senior management teams that are most aligned with millennials in terms of purpose, culture and professional development are likely to attract and retain the best millennial talent and... achieve better financial performance," states the report. "Loyalty must be earned, and the vast majority of millennials are prepared to move, and move quickly, for a better workplace experience."

See, one of the root causes of turnover today is that younger workers aren't afraid to leave. For them, a job has to be fair, a win-win situation, or there's no deal—they will get up and walk away. There's nothing to keep them in your organization if they see more conflict than connection inside, and there's a big wide world of possibilities just waiting for them outside of your company. That means it's vital for companies to learn how to create an atmosphere that encourages those win-win opportunities, and that gives everyone a reason to stay.

Addressing employee turnover and retention is neither simple nor easy—I'll be the first to admit that. It can be a lot of work to uncover and address underlying management problems and culture issues, and clients often ask me what will happen if they invest all of that time and effort and their employees still leave.

So, if you're thinking the same thing, let me ask you this: What will happen if you don't invest in your people? They'll leave anyway. Or, worse, they'll mentally quit, and stay.

Here's the bottom line: many companies are losing or misusing good people and bleeding them out somewhere down the line. Their leaders may be adept at producing great quarterly projections for their growing business, but there doesn't seem to be the same urgency or understanding when it comes to predicting or solving the problem of high employee turnover. And even when they are aware of the high cost of hiring and training new employees, companies can't fully measure the intangible cost of lost productivity, missed opportunities, and poor morale.

If you're reading this book, you probably do understand all of this very well. But there's still one more hurdle: if you don't know *why* your people are leaving, you won't know what you need to change to entice them to stay.

Misdiagnosing the Problem

"Diagnostic errors affect more than 12 million Americans each year and likely cause more harm to patients than all other medical errors combined," writes the Society to Improve Diagnosis in Medicine. "Best estimates also suggest that diagnostic error wastes as much as $50–100 billion per year on inappropriate testing, wrong treatments, and malpractice lawsuits."[7]

Scary, right? Why am I telling you this? Because misdiagnosis happens in the business world too. It might not kill your business, but it can cause lasting harm and unnecessary expense. I've seen organizations spend valuable time and money trying to fix issues that are actually just symptoms, while the real problem goes unidentified.

These are the main trends I've observed over five years of undercover work:

- A company recognizes that turnover is a problem, but uses one-size-fits-all solutions based on generational stereotypes like "millennials like free food and ping-pong tables" instead of determining their people's real needs.

- They recognize the turnover, but rely on employee surveys for insights—meaning the feedback they're getting is cautious and filtered, and likely not the whole truth.

- They believe high turnover is inevitable and think, "Why waste money on people who are going to leave anyway?" So they don't bother to provide their people with opportunities for professional development and growth.

- They believe that turnover doesn't matter—they see their employees as cogs that can be easily replaced to keep the wheels turning. They aren't so much misdiagnosing as not diagnosing at all.

- They try to save money by hiring from outside the company rather than promoting from within (and giving raises with those promotions).

- Or, they try to save money by not providing much in the way of benefits, despite the fact that the incredible cost of health insurance in the U.S. means that benefits can be as or even more important than salaries to many employees.

So many companies are trying to solve the wrong problems—fighting the smoke, not the flames. Yes, you need to get rid of the smoke if you want to breathe, but the smoke will be there until the fire is put out.

Will your misdiagnosis cause your organization to fail? Perhaps not, but it *can* stifle your company's growth. Misdiagnosis is a mistake you can't afford, especially when employees are ready to leave the moment something better comes along.

So how can you diagnose a problem correctly? It begins with you—the leader.

Why Engagement Matters

We've gone deep into the costs of turnover, and now it's time to look at the flipside: the vast benefits your company can reap from higher rates of engagement and retention. They might seem obvious—after all, who wants to go through the cost and process of finding, hiring, and training new employees if you don't have to? But there's so much more to it than saving time and saving money. Let me dive into our real-world research to give you a few examples of what high employee engagement can mean:

- "Richie" worked as a server at a very popular sit-down restaurant that's part of a chain found throughout the U.S. He was an immediate standout to me, because he was the best server I had ever had: his attention to detail and customer service was flawless. I asked him what it was like to work at the restaurant, and he said, "I love my job, and I love what I get to do." He told me he had been serving at that location for eight years. That felt like a long time considering the high turnover rates in the food and beverage industry. I asked what had kept him there for so long. "My manager," he said. "Nancy" had worked as a manager in the food and beverage industry for twenty-five years. I could see for myself that her kindness and charisma was contagious, and that the connection between them meant more than a paycheck. I asked her what her secret was for

---

Don't we all want to feel valued in the place where we spend so much of our time?

---

the great relationship she had with her staff, and she simply said, "I just love 'em. And I just... listen to them."

- BambooHR, a company that makes human resources
  management software, has won numerous awards for
  workplace culture: Great Place to Work certification for
  the years 2012–2020; 2019 Best 50 Workplaces in Technology from *Fortune*; 2020 Employees' Choice Best Places
  to Work from Glassdoor; 2019 Best Software Companies from G2—to name a few. The company has grown

to six hundred employees without needing any venture capital; it is a profitable, privately held company with no debt. Cassie Whitlock, head of HR, lists two measures of business success: "We are able to find the talent we need... If we couldn't do that, the whole thing would collapse," she told me. And they are uniquely successful as a business. "For a SaaS company, we break all the metrics, hands down. We have a great product, and our people execute." Cassie said that clients stay not only because of the quality of their software, but also because their people are motivated to provide great support and service at a deep, caring level. "That's what employees are experiencing in the office and it just spills over through the phone, through email, and becomes an extension of our culture," she explained.

- "Curt," an employee at a popular fast-food chain that specializes in burgers, loved his job. I spent a few days frequenting his location undercover, because every employee I spoke with answered with such enthusiasm about their job, a fairly uncommon response in that industry. I finally asked Curt what was so great about his workplace, and he responded with the name of his manager. Oddly enough, every employee mentioned "Ashley" in one way or another. Curt was so proud of Ashley that he insisted I meet her, and brought her out to say hi. Ashley had been the manager in that location for over five years, having previously managed at another fast-food franchise for three years before that. When she left her old job for this one, four employees followed her, including Curt. *Four.* She hadn't pressured them, but simply invited them to be a part of her new team, and they gladly did so. When I asked Curt why he and his co-workers left a better paying job to follow Ashley to this one, he said, "We are a family. We are a team. Getting paid more doesn't really outweigh the happiness of being part of a job and a team that has each other's backs."

While these examples address some of the intangible benefits of having engaged employees—Richie's respect for his manager keeps his service at the highest caliber; BambooHR's customer service is off the charts; Curt's fast-food location is full of employees who love being at their job—the same results can't come from those who don't feel engaged or connected to their work (or those they work with). Disengaged employees will undermine your workplace and make it impossible to build anything close to the kinds of cultures I've just described, and the financial consequences are not to be overlooked, either. "According to Gallup, disengaged employees have 37% higher absenteeism, 18% lower productivity and 15% lower profitability," writes Karlyn Borysenko in *Forbes*. "When that translates into dollars, you're looking at the cost of 34% of a disengaged employee's annual salary."[8]

And having loyal and engaged employees makes work more enjoyable for everyone, along with any benefits it adds to your bottom line. Don't we all want to work with people who like their jobs and who respect and appreciate both their co-workers and their employers? Don't we all want to feel valued in the place where we spend so much of our time?

Here's what we know: If your employees don't feel valued, and if they don't share—or even know—your company's vision and how it helps them live a more fulfilling life, they will go elsewhere. Your job as a leader is to show them—every day—why they should stay. That comes down to making sure they're engaged, and that's what I'm going to show you how to do throughout the rest of this book.

MASTERING YOUR MOMENTS

Question #1: When was the last time you lost an employee? What was their reason for leaving?

Question #2: When you lost that employee, was it expected or was it a surprise? Why?

Question #3: Did you learn anything from the departing employee that could help you retain others? If so, what?

Challenge: Build employee loyalty

Determine the one thing you'd most like to improve in your leadership. You can do this by defining what being a leader means for you. Think about the good leaders you have experienced or read about. Be detailed. How did they treat those they led? What did their interactions with employees look like? What kind of connection did they have?

The people you hire create the foundation of your company. Ultimately, **they will be your greatest assets**.

— 3 —

CREATING YOUR DREAM TEAM

You can have the best strategy and the best building in the world, but if you don't have the hearts and minds of the people who work with you, none of it comes to life.

RENEE WEST

AVING A LOYAL and engaged workforce starts first, of course, with getting those people into your company to begin with, and helping them work well together. If you're a sports fan, you probably know the origins of the term "Dream Team"—the original Dream Team was the 1992 U.S. men's Olympic basketball team, led by head coach Chuck Daly. And if you're not familiar with the concept of a Dream Team, I highly recommend the 1996 documentary *Space Jam*.

But in all seriousness, what earned Daly's team the nickname wasn't just its members, which included some of the greatest ever to play the sport—Michael Jordan, Magic Johnson, Karl Malone—but also their cohesiveness. Their individual excellence worked to challenge every member of the team to do better, thus lifting the team up as a whole. That combination of performance, mutual respect, and support—people playing their positions well and working together toward a common goal—is what we're looking for in our own employee Dream Teams.

Engagement becomes so much easier when you have your Dream Team—they are all working to engage each other as much as you are working to engage them. When each member of the teams knows they are performing at their best, they won't want to leave.

The Four Principles of Hiring for a Dream Team

So where do you start? Step one is to hire the right people in the first place. This is such an important aspect of employee engagement that I'm going to say it again: hiring the right people for your business is an absolute *must*.

In my experience with the Undercover Millennial program, I've seen so many things that successful organizations have done to keep their employees from leaving. But some of the best decisions have been made during the hiring process. I've examined this hiring process, and the practices that the most successful leaders have followed as they hired new employees for their companies. What I've learned is that it comes down to four basic principles:

1 Hire the right person, not the convenient person.
2 Hire internally when possible.
3 Hire for the ABCs: attitude, behavior, and character.
4 Let your employees focus on what they do best.

If you'll remember, in the last chapter I shared the negative effects that a high turnover rate can have on a company, with three-quarters of turnover among the employees we've interviewed being traceable back to poor management. That means the remaining 25 percent can be attributed to other causes, and a big part of that is poor hiring decisions. Having an employee leave a job they should never have been hired for is an expensive mistake—averaging, like the turnover we discussed before, about $15,000 for each bad hire, according to CareerBuilder.[1] Ouch.

If you think that's costly, consider that not all bad hires choose to leave. Some stay, and simply remain disengaged. That costs the organization in other ways: poor performance, lower productivity, lower revenue. That's all a lot of pain from one bad hiring decision. So let's break down those four basic hiring principles, so you can get the right people in the right positions moving in the right direction.

1. Hire the right person, not the convenient person

A common mistake we often come across in the Undercover Millennial program is settling on the wrong employee—or the wrong person in a position of leadership—in order to meet a looming deadline. This is a backward view of the workplace, in which deadlines are more important than the work you're striving to accomplish. How many times have you hired an employee as quickly as possible because your workload was too much, or the pressures of feeling under-staffed made it seem like that was your biggest problem to solve? Perhaps, in that moment, it was.

Let me give you an airplane analogy (you'll see as this book goes along that I have a bit of a thing for aviation). Before a pilot prepares to land an aircraft, the first thing they do is to put down the landing gear and make sure the parking brake is released. This lets the wind get the wheels spinning, which is critical to do before landing so that they don't have to go from zero to 250 miles per hour in one second. With the wheels already in motion, you get a nice smooth touchdown.

It's the same principle for onboarding: a hire who has the right experience, abilities, and attitude is like a wheel that's already spinning, making for a smooth and seamless arrival. All of the most successful business leaders we've worked with take the time to find the right fit, even when it's difficult. As Cassie Whitlock from BambooHR told me:

> We make a deliberate choice to wait to hire the right person, and sometimes that's painful. Once we had a departure on our team, and I was the only person with the technical expertise to fill in for that role on a day-to-day basis. I was doing some double duty, and I could have just been desperate and said, "I don't care; get me help in here." And sometimes I want to do that. But I recognize that I have a duty to the rest of my team to make sure we bring on somebody with the right fit.

The people you hire create the foundation of your company. Ultimately, they will be your greatest assets, so choose carefully. *Do not settle.* Don't let the short-term demands of your business dictate who will determine your long-term success. Take the time to find the right fit. It might not be the first, second, third, or fourth candidate you interview—it might not even be the tenth. But the right person *will* come along—and I can promise you that your patience will pay off in the long run.

Okay, you might be thinking: "But where do I find the right people? They don't seem to be anywhere!" or "I don't need any more employees right now." That may be true, but this mentality is a reactive one. If you want the right people to help build your company, stop operating under the perception that any effort to change or improve your business can happen only when it's forced upon you, or when you have no other choice but to start looking for more employees. Instead, remember that innovative organizations are proactive. They are *always* on the lookout for great people. BambooHR offers this invitation on their careers page, after the list of open positions: "Don't see the job you're looking for? That's okay! Send your resume anyway, and we'll call you when something comes up."

Is it possible that you'll still wind up short staffed once in a while? Of course. But having a mindset of "always be recruiting" will make it easier for you to hire the people you want, instead of the ones you think you desperately need.

2. Hire internally when possible

The smartest place to look for a new hire is within your own company. More often than not—and despite what they want prospective employees to believe—companies hire from the outside because they believe it will save money.

Hiring younger or less experienced employees so you can pay them less than you'd pay to promote from within might be cheaper in the short run, but it's not an effective policy in the long run. Our undercover research shows that hiring from outside has two immediate consequences for existing employees:

- It discourages them from seeing any potential for future growth within the company.

- It begins to disengage them from their work.

The benefits of promoting from within far outweigh the prospect of a cheap outside hire. Consider these unique skills that you'll find in someone who already works for your company:

- They have already connected and developed meaningful and trusting relationships with people in your organization.

- They have a firm grasp on the inner workings and culture of your company, right from the first day in their new position.

Most importantly, though, hiring from the inside will help your people feel excited and empowered about the career potential they'll find in your organization—and that means increased engagement, and increased loyalty.

So where do you look to find the right people in your ranks? The easiest place to start is to ask your current employees if they know anyone who'd be great for the role you want to fill. Internships, too, can be a goldmine, if you approach them right. Jeanette Bennett, founder and editor-in-chief at Bennett Communications (you'll hear more from her later) told me that she takes the hiring of interns very seriously, because each is a possible future employee. At the time we talked, Jeanette had permanently hired about ten interns after their internship term was over.

There's a middle ground, too, between hiring outside and hiring inside, and that's through a referral program. Giving your employees the opportunity to bring in people they know, like, and trust can help maintain your organization's culture, and further increase retention. Your referral rate is a good indicator of your retention rate: if your employees want to bring people in, that tells you that you're on the right track in keeping them happy and engaged.

There's one thing to keep in mind: remember that this second principle is "Hire internally *when possible.*" If you've considered your internal employees, but still feel that the best candidate for the job is from an external source, then great! That keeps right in line with principle number 1. Find the balance, and make the best decision for your company.

Do they fit your culture? Will the position challenge them? Can they find purpose here? **These are the things that will determine the right hire.**

3. Hire for the ABCs: attitude, behavior, and character

We have found that hiring for these three qualities is at least as important as hiring for technical ability. In some fields, it might even be more important. (Technical skills can be taught if necessary, but character is harder to shape.) In the past, hiring managers typically focused on where candidates have worked and what they've done, how many degrees they have, or where they went to school. But the working market is changing—creativity, adaptability, collaboration, teamwork, and the ability to communicate are now considered essential for many jobs.

These skills are difficult to assess from résumés, especially when you consider that a high percentage of résumés are, shall we say, inaccurate. (A 2017 report by HireRight found that 85 percent of employers have caught a job applicant lying on their applications.[2]) Catching someone in a lie tells you something about that person's character, so that, at least, is one way to eliminate someone from your pool of candidates. Integrity seems like an important requirement for just about any job (outside of politics of course).

Checking an applicant's references is a good place to start. Let me give you a couple of examples of what other business leaders have done to feel out applicants during the hiring process. "Michelle," the hiring manager at a high-profile firm, told me how she always calls references, even though they're often not helpful beyond verifying the basics. "Occasionally there's just a tone or there's just a hint, even if they're saying something nice like, 'Oh, they're a hard worker,'" she said. "But I sense something."

In other words: listen to your gut. After that, it's time for interviews. Preferably more than one, and preferably including other people in your organization or on the specific team that's looking to add a new member.

Use interviews to learn what you can about the candidate. Pam Jarvis is the overseeing office manager for a chain of very successful pediatric and family medicine clinics. For seven years, the company has maintained a yearly employee retention rate of over 70 percent—an impressive track record. "When I interview people, I'm all about getting them to talk about themselves and their experiences with work," she told me when I asked her about her hiring process. "They'll offer up exactly what you need to know if you just give them the opportunity."

To draw people out, Pam asks three questions:

"If you could pick the ideal job and it had all the things you need, what would that entail? What are the things that you would have on your list?" People might respond with "I need to have a positive environment" or "a boss that listens to me" or "employees that are kind" or "co-workers that I can get along with." This information can help you determine whether someone is a good fit and how you can help them get what they need.

"Tell me about a place you've worked where you wish that things had been a little bit different, and what you would do to fix it." People will either start listing complaints—"my manager was terrible, and he didn't listen to us"; "he didn't care about me"; "she wouldn't let me have time off"; "I was always late and then they fired me"—or they'll discuss what they did to try to improve a bad situation. Among other things, Pam wants to know: were they invested in their job, or when it got ugly, did they just fail?

"Who is somebody that you really loved working with? And why did you love working with them?" Answers might be "because we always went to lunch," or "he helped me with a work issue," or "I could go to her with problems." That last answer is particularly helpful because it tells you that the person is willing to ask for help if they feel in over their head, or take advice if they don't understand how to do something. "We live in such a shame-based society that people are scared to ask for help," Pam explained. "They'd rather make some mistake and try to cover it up instead of saying, 'I screwed up and I need some help. Will somebody help me fix this?'"

"Jonathan," a manager for over twenty-five years at a retail chain, told me that he pays close attention to what new candidates are looking for. Do they need full-time hours? Are they in school and can only work in the evenings? Is working on weekends off limits, and if so, is that something the company can navigate? Do they communicate their scheduling limits clearly? Even if they have good qualities, not every candidate will be a perfect fit, and your honest evaluation of what your company needs will help determine how much flexibility you can offer.

There's more to finding that right fit than what can be seen in a résumé or expressed in a cover letter. Often, the kind of connection an employee has with an organization can be seen from the very first interview. Do they fit your culture? Will the position challenge them? Can they find purpose here? These are the things that will determine the right hire.

One last thing to remember: the process isn't just about finding the person who is the best hire. It's also about putting that right hire in the position that will bring out their best. And that brings us to the final principle.

4. Let your employees focus on what they do best

The exceptional leaders that we have met in our research understand that hiring and developing great employees is about putting people in the places where they'll shine, and where their strengths and passions can best serve the work they do. It's always evident when an employee is shining where they stand—working in their element, and doing what they do best.

If you want an employee to stay actively engaged, make sure the tasks you assign them are aligned with the strengths they naturally possess. I don't mean to imply that you shouldn't push or challenge your people to try new things or expand their skill sets, but more that you should ask yourself where you could put them and who you could put them with to best utilize those strengths.

Developing your people is a fundamental principle of successful mentorship—and it's something we'll get into more, starting in the next chapter. But finding a way to also tap into a person's natural abilities will improve their performance, increase their engagement, and allow you to focus better on developing their unique skills.

When I was undercover in a major pet store chain, I found that every employee was placed in a specific department based upon their love and expertise. Employees who loved reptiles and had the specialized knowledge needed to care for them were placed with the reptiles and amphibians. People who had an affinity for fish and aquatic animals were placed in the aquarium section—and so on. Because of this, the animals received better care and the customers who adopted them were educated properly about what their new pets would need to thrive.

I know it seems like common sense—of course you would put somebody who knows more about snakes in charge of the snakes—but, for some reason, that simplicity gets blurred when a company is scrambling to fill a position. That's not necessarily a disaster: at times, an employee's best position isn't ones they start in. Sometimes it can take a while to discover an employee's strengths and the best position for them.

But the time it takes to understand where an employee best thrives is not the issue; the real issue is the uncertainty that prevents you from taking action once you know that a move is needed.

Don't be afraid of change, or the perceived effort you think it will take to move your people around. Once, when undercover, I met an employee, "Hilary," who had worked for over five years in a successful clothing department store. She spent a lot of time working in the back of the store, in shipping. Her manager had noticed how she organized some of their back inventory in a way that was much more visually pleasing than even the merchandise that was out on the floor. He decided to move her to the front of the store, allowing her to use her unique organization and styling skills to create beautiful visual presentations. Hilary eventually gained recognition from upper executives during a corporate visit. Now, she is known and respected within the corporation, and their store looks immaculate, which only adds to the experience of any customer that walks in.

This aspect of hiring requires a bit of work on your part to make the effort to understand a job candidate as best as you can. In our research, we have found that the most personable employers asked their prospects (internal or external) questions like these:

- What is your life's dream?
- What is it that you want to achieve in life?
- What means the most to you?
- What do you want to accomplish in the workplace?

These might feel quite personal, and not everyone will want to answer them—maybe not until they know you better, maybe not ever—and that's fine. Your intention is not to trample people's boundaries, but to communicate interest and caring. A big part of your role is to be a mentor, but it's hard to be a mentor if your employees don't even know what they can expect from you.

Finding out what a potential employee wants to achieve is an important part of determining whether they're a good fit for the job. If you pay attention and ask the right questions, prospective employees will reveal the areas they specialize in and where they can best benefit your organization.

Remember Jeanette Bennett from Bennett Communications? She once interviewed a prospect, "Dean," for a position in her company. Dean told her he wanted to come on board, and that he wanted to open an ad agency as a new line of business within the organization. He had the chops—in his previous position, he took on ad buying for several of his clients. Jeanette liked the idea, and she worked with Dean to figure out how they could make it happen. They launched the agency as a unique entity within her organization, and split the profits.

If you can better understand the ambitions, wants, and motivations of an employee, you can match those ambitions and skill sets with your company's needs, creating more opportunities for you to help connect that employee to their dreams. Over time, you will have not only created experts out of your individual team members using their own capacities, you will also have developed engaged team members who feel valued and supported.

Expand Your Understanding of Disability

Occasionally, while undercover, I come across employees who have visible disabilities, ranging from visual impairment to developmental disabilities like Down syndrome to physical disabilities that require mobility aids like canes or wheelchairs. For many hiring managers, these individuals aren't the first who come to mind when they imagine their team—and that's a shame, and a true missed opportunity to tap into some incredible talent.

Dave Hennessey is the CEO of TURN Community Services, an organization that provides program services for more than eight hundred adult individuals with developmental disabilities. He has a unique perspective from working daily with these individuals, and it echoes my own experience from going undercover. "There's a certain spirit that people with disabilities can bring to the workplace," he told me. "It brings a stronger sense of community. It strengthens culture. It gives people the opportunity to serve someone else and brings a sense of camaraderie."

There's something special about leaders who can see and value these opportunities instead of fearing the limitations, and the benefits of that vision are always clearly apparent to me when I visit their workplaces. I saw it when I met "Drew," who worked in a tire store franchise, and when I was welcomed in by "Bryan," a greeter at a cellphone storefront— both men with Down syndrome who bring a lot of value to their employers. The spirit and community you felt in these organizations was palpable, not only for the customers and for me as an outsider, but for the other employees as well.

Now, not all disabilities will lend themselves to every type of work that you need accomplished. It's not discriminatory, it's just fact. But if you encounter a great person who can't fill a specific need due to a disability, I bet you could find another place in your organization where they could thrive—think back to earlier in this chapter, where I talked about hiring for the person, not the skills. An equal opportunity mindset requires that you broaden your understanding of ability and of disability, and to consider that most, if not all, of the people on your existing team have their own unique talents and limitations. As Dave Hennessey pointed out to me, "Everybody has disabilities. Everybody. Some of our disabilities are just more visible than others." From my years of experience in observing teams and workplaces, I could not agree more.

When you do bring on an individual with a disability, there are countless resources available to help your organization transition to become a more accommodating culture and space. The U.S. Department of Labor supports several initiatives that can help employers who are interested in hiring individuals with disabilities, including guidance and tools for interviewing and onboarding. The Job Accommodation Network is also a great resource, providing free, expert advice on workplace accommodations that may be necessary to assist qualified individuals with disabilities with maximizing their productivity once on board.

A Sense of Community

You've followed the four principles of good hiring, you've taken a fresh look at your team to find potential talent that's been hidden in plain sight, you've found new sources of outside hires that could make a great fit, you've refined your interviewing techniques, and you've learned to place people where they will do their best work. Now you have a new question: How do all of these people come together to create a positive, high-performing culture?

Consider this thought from strategy expert Freek Vermeulen, writing in the *Harvard Business Review*:[3]

At the end of the day, organizations are collections of people; this means that superior organizations need more effective ways for them to cooperate and work toward a common goal. As the famous management professor Henry Mintzberg noted: "Think of the organizations you most admire. I'll bet that front and center is a powerful sense of community."

Once you have the right combination of people on your team, your next job is to help them connect not just with you but also with each other—that's the secret glue that turns a good team into a Dream Team. While undercover, I once spoke to a man whose favorite manager used to buy donuts every Tuesday for the whole team. Everyone would come in early on that day just for those donuts. The manager retired, and at the goodbye party the man asked his manager, "Why the donuts?" The manager's reply: "It was never about the donuts. It was always about the chance to connect, and the chance to get to know each other and engage in each other's lives."

It's as simple as that, and it's more complicated, too. In the chapters to come, I'll break down many of the different ways you can help your people connect, show them how they can rely on each other, and facilitate the sense of trust and teamwork that will get them pulling together in the right direction.

MASTERING YOUR MOMENTS

Question #1: Think of an employee in your own organization who may be disruptive to the team. Are they in the right position for both their own growth and the company's? What needs to happen to get them into the right position within your organization?

Question #2: What are the questions you can implement in your hiring and interview process that will help you place the right employees in the right positions, and help them reach their goals?

Question #3: Do you currently have openings in your organization that need to be filled? If so, think to your current employees. Do any of them possess the skills and potential to be promoted in that direction?

Challenge: Create your own Dream Team

Think of the kind of people you want working for you, and write down their traits. Now, attune your attention and start actively seeking out people who have those traits. They may already be in your organization; if so, great—now make sure you have them in positions that bring out their strengths. If you need to look outside the company, put in the time to recruit not only those with great talent, but also those who can actually improve your team's dynamic. Everyone on your team may have talent, but that doesn't matter much if they can't work together.

Once you have found the right person, do whatever it takes to get them on your team.

I heard the **gut-wrenching sound of metal banging against metal**—*bam!* I didn't need to look; I knew what had happened.

— 4 —

THE MENTOR MANAGER

You are not here merely to make a living. You are here in order to enable the world to live more simply, with greater vision, with a finer spirit of hope and achievement. You are here to enrich the world, and you impoverish yourself if you forget the errand.

WOODROW WILSON

WHAT DOES it mean to love your job? This is a hot topic, as the idea of loving your job isn't something that can be packaged in a box—it's very subjective, and everybody has an opinion about it. Some would argue that loving your job means to be "on fire" each day, to wake up each morning excited to go to work. Others would say that we need to learn to love what we already do instead of always trying to find the perfect job.

Tim Grover, author of *Relentless: From Good to Great to Unstoppable*, says: "You don't have to love the hard work. You just have to crave the end result so much that the hard work becomes irrelevant."[1] I love how this puts the emphasis on the result. Every job out there will have aspects that aren't enjoyable. A teacher may love working with students and having the chance to educate and shape young minds, but that doesn't mean they have to love dealing with unhappy parents. A surgeon may love the chance to alleviate pain or improve quality of life, but that doesn't mean they love the mounds of paperwork, charting, and dictation that come with it. The point is, when you're doing work that makes you crave the result, the negative aspects of that work become more tolerable.

Remember last chapter when I said I had a thing for planes and aviation? When I was young, aviation was the thing that made me so connected to the result that any negative aspects of the field were almost invisible (*almost* being key, as you'll see). Ever since I was a kid, I've wanted to fly planes, helicopters, just about anything that could get up in the air, and even some things that shouldn't. When I'd imagine being grown up, I'd see myself sporting a leather aviator jacket and gold-framed Ray-Bans model 3025 (the "Aviator Classic" sunglasses—think *Top Gun*, my all-time favorite film).

So when I got a job as a lineman at the local regional airport, I loved it. The rumbling vibrations of rotors overhead as aircraft landed and took off, the thrill of seeing them thunder by mere feet off the ground, and the smell—a mixture of fuel, sweat, and grease. It was all heaven for a high school kid like me.

I was in charge of fueling the airplanes, pulling them in and out of the hangars, polishing and cleaning some of the aircraft, and making sure the airport was safe and in order. It was not easy work, especially given that I was trying to balance it with homework, extracurricular activities, dating, a social life, and chores at home, but every day I pushed myself to show my boss that I deserved to be there. Just as Tim Grover said, I didn't mind the hard work and long hours— twelve-hour shifts that started at 6 a.m.—because my craving for the result overshadowed everything else. In my off time, I took flying lessons. I was determined to be the youngest pilot in the state, a goal I eventually accomplished.

Because of my enthusiasm and hard work, I was entrusted with more and more responsibility. One day, I was asked to back a plane out of a hangar, something I routinely did. No big deal. But as I maneuvered the plane out, I heard the gut-wrenching sound of metal banging against metal—*bam!* I didn't need to look; I knew what had happened. My heart sank.

Jumping down, I ran to the side of the plane to assess the damage. The plane had hit the hangar doorway and bent the wingtip. I was mortified; I had been around long enough to know that this was a very expensive mistake. Frantic, I racked my brain for anything I could do to make it better. Maybe, I thought, I could find a way to make up for it—something that would assure my boss this would *never* happen again. But it was no use; I came up empty. Reluctantly, I went to inform my boss.

Fessing up to the accident was especially daunting because my manager and I did not have the best relationship. He took no interest in me and didn't seem to care about anything so long as I was on time in the morning and got my work done. He never noticed the care I took in my job. He only saw numbers on a spreadsheet registering clocked-in, clocked-out, and gave no attention to the fact that I excelled at my work while balancing all the other aspects of my young life.

Maybe if he'd known the passion I had for aviation, his response would have been different. But this supervisor had a "my way or the highway" management style that left no room for mistakes—and therefore no room for learning. I was let go immediately. Because of one incalculable mistake and the intolerance of one boss, a lifelong dream suddenly felt squelched in a day.

Managing with Empathy and Expectations

Good leadership requires empathy—this is wisdom that has been espoused by human relationship experts from Oprah Winfrey to Daniel Goleman. A manager's ability to relate to and connect with their staff is as important to an employee's engagement as that manager's level of expectations and standards. Together, these two components have been a common thread in the four types of managers we find across virtually every organization (more on those types soon).

In fact, these two factors—their level of connection to their employees, and the level of expectations/standards they set for their employees—have been so commonly linked to successful workplaces in our research that we now use them to assess managers. What do I mean by "connection"? Connection is the link that forms when people experience a consistent, high level of trust, love, empathy, kindness, and care. This link can look different for each person and each relationship—some want to share their life dreams, others are more private but still appreciate being valued for who they are. (You can show interest without prying; take your cues from each person, and remember that developing relationships takes time.) The spectrum of connection is limitless, and always unique.

In addition to connection, employees value clear expectations and an understanding of the rules and standards. It's safe to say that most employees are familiar with their job descriptions when they enter an organization. Unfortunately, however, many don't know the finer details of what's expected of them. Yes, their job titles might be clear, but if new hires don't receive the orientation and training they need, then the logistics of why, when, and how they're supposed to take care of their duties might remain a mystery.

Connection is the
link that forms when
people experience
a consistent, high level
of **trust, love, empathy,
kindness, and care**.

Your expectations can be as high or as low as you want them to be, but if they are not clear, your ship will sail nowhere.

Many of the tools I offer throughout this book are designed to help you connect with your employees, and to communicate in a way that puts you both on the same page. Connection and clarity of expectations may be difficult to quantify in a tangible way, but looking at management through the lens of these factors is a very effective predictor of specific behaviors in a company's employees. It's so predictable, in fact, that we can chart the outcome.

The Four Types of Managers

In our undercover work and the conversations with employees that involves, we've heard repeated and consistent descriptions of four management styles—and each can be placed on a spectrum of the two critical leadership factors of *expectations/standards* and *connection/empathy.*

Type of Manager	Expectations & Standards	Connection & Empathy	Result
The Removed Manager	Low	Low	Disengagement
The Buddy Manager	Low	High	Entitlement
The Controlling Manager	High	Low	Rebellion and pushback
The Mentor Manager	High	High	Respect and loyalty

Every type of manager on this spectrum creates their own unique results, whether they intend to or not. Let's look at each of them in turn.

1. The Removed Manager
(low expectations, low connection)

The Removed Manager is, as the name implies, completely removed from the organization—emotionally, and often physically. This manager is either not present at all or stays in their office or the store's back room. Doing only what's needed to get by, they don't help out on the sales floor or pitch in when someone needs a hand. They certainly don't do any manual labor, like changing tires or cleaning bathrooms. For whatever reason—perhaps boredom, perhaps burnout—they view leadership as a burden. Because they are disengaged themselves, they struggle to connect with their people; it's not surprising that many of their employees are also disengaged. Removed managers often say things like "I can't get my employees to engage at work" or "They just run through the motions to get a paycheck" or "They wouldn't change even if I told them to."

As a result of removed management, employees feel rejected and massively undervalued. Usually it's not long before they're searching for a new place of employment.

2. The Buddy Manager
(low expectations, high connection)

This manager can also be called the Rescuing Manager. The combination of low expectations and high connection means the employees end up doing more managing than the actual manager. They feel cared for, but sense a lack of leadership and authority.

The Buddy Manager is just that—a buddy. Approval and friendship is more important to them than leading and empowering each of their employees to be better. You can often hear the Buddy Manager say things like "I want to be here for you. Anything you need, you let me know" or "Sure, take the rest of the week off." Consequently, when it comes to standards, the laxness creates entitlement. The Buddy Manager might treat some people differently from others, often making exceptions when performance standards aren't met. That soon leads to exceptions for everyone, and where does that get you? Nowhere.

One of the worst things that can happen to your authority as a manager is for an employee to become a "great friend" and begin to take advantage of the relationship. It starts innocently enough, but soon they're showing up late for work, not completing their work efficiently, and seeing how far they can stretch standards. And they'll expect you to tolerate it because *that's what friends do.* (Tip: this isn't actually what real friends do.)

We have often found Buddy Managers in the retail, hospitality, technology, and food and beverage industries. These fields are ones in which managers are most often overseeing employees who are of similar ages. In one company we visited undercover, employees consistently made comments about how their bosses were "homies" and really nice, and how they could do whatever they wanted. Coincidentally, that company is no longer in business.

This doesn't mean you shouldn't have great relationships with your employees—you absolutely should! Nor does it mean that your company is heading for trouble if your employees and your managers are near the same age. But when a manager's relationship with their employees takes precedence over the good of the company, that's when problems arise. The Buddy Manager will let friendship or fear of disapproval get in the way of making tough decisions. Employees should always have a voice, but they need to know and understand that you are the leader. Connection is important, but so are boundaries.

3. The Controlling Manager
(high expectations, low connection)

This is the "my way or the highway" manager—just like my old boss at the airplane hangar. Their rigid and forceful management style results in rebellion, outward defiance, and variations of deliberate rule breaking. Collaboration is low, and punishment is high. Employees get written up or put on probation, breaks are canceled, pay is reduced or threatened, and people are fired.

The Controlling Manager operates without much care for their employees as individuals, and they believe that allowing their workers to receive a paycheck is appreciation enough. Employees might hear "Be glad you have a job" or "Put your head down and get to work—do that, and we won't have any issues."

"Mark," an employee at a tech startup, shared his experience about his current supervisor, who had a heavy hand: "It was ugly. We had all this control and then all of a sudden this new manager said, 'Nothing is done without my approval. And we'll do it my way or the highway.' He lost a lot of people. And it was rough for a long time."

Gallup polls[2] show that the manager of a company accounts for at least 70 percent of variance in employee engagement. Further, only 30 percent of U.S. employees are engaged at work, and only 13 percent worldwide. This disengagement—caused by bad management—costs a company in many ways. It can result in loss of productivity from disgruntled employees,

---

Your title might make you a supervisor but **your people will decide if you're a mentor.**

---

in theft or purposeful mistakes because of employee retaliation, or the replacement costs of a new hire when an employee can no longer handle the difficulties of working for a bad manager. You can't afford to have managers like this—or to be one of these managers yourself.

4. The Mentor Manager (high expectations, high connection)

This is where the magic happens! Employees who work for a Mentor Manager give respect and loyalty, and engage with their work and their co-workers on the highest level. Mentor Managers are able to communicate an employee's worth and potential so well that the person begins to see those things within themselves (if they didn't already).

A Mentor Manager is somebody who is constantly striving to be with their people, asking the questions and making *deposits of trust*. Just like with a bank account, if you deposit a lot—connection, leadership, inspiration—you can ask for more in return. These deposits of trust create respect and understanding, allowing your workplace to flourish in the way it needs to.

It's important to remember that, as a leader in your organization, you are being watched. People are waiting to see what you'll do and how you'll handle each challenge. Being a Mentor Manager is about connection and the ability to truly relate to your people, especially in difficult situations. Many corporations are great at developing people, but it's just as important to work on developing your connections with those people. How do you start? It's not so much about connecting to your employees as it is about being somebody who your employees want to connect to. Your title might make you a supervisor but your people will decide if you're a mentor. This is why becoming a Mentor Manager is the most valuable skill set you can acquire.

Traditional Leaders vs. Mentor Managers

Since you have associated with another human being at least once in your life, you know firsthand that you can't change another person. Nobody can. Each of us can only change ourselves. But as a leader, you *can* influence, motivate, and inspire someone in such a positive way that it moves them to change their own life.

In our years of running the Undercover Millennial program, we've interviewed thousands of millennials and younger workers about their jobs—what they loved, why they loved it; what they didn't love, why they didn't love it; and so on. The most prominent answer we heard from satisfied employees was that they loved their boss.

We rarely hear employees compliment a leader's ability to organize, make a solid meeting agenda, or increase productivity. Instead, they praise their ability to guide, connect, advocate, and empathize. For the employees, these intangible skills are the foundation of everything that is good and right— and it works the opposite way too. When employees hate their jobs, it's still their leaders we hear about most. Interestingly, what changes between these two situations is the language. When employees hate their job, they talk about their *manager*. When they love their job, they talk about their *mentor*.

What we've learned in our research is that there is a very clear distinction between mentorship and traditional leadership. Both have characteristics that are valuable and necessary, but they are not the same thing. So, what are the qualities of a mentor? We can throw around words like "guide," "connect," "advocate," and "empathize" all we want, but the best way to understand it is perhaps to start by describing what it is not.

The attributes of a *traditional leader* look like this:

- They are the visionary—they set the tone, pace, attitude, and direction for a business. Typically, their employees are following their agenda, goals, parameters, and values. Traditional leaders prefer employees who fit the dynamics of what they are trying to accomplish. The leader's job is to focus on where the ship is going.

- They have to focus on the big picture. Because of this, they require accountability from others to meet production and marketing goals—employees must honor the vision of the company.

- They are the financial decision maker. They have hard decisions, and often have to shed the dead weight of employees, products, and programs that aren't working so their ship can move faster and more effectively.

- They stand in the front and lead, while everyone else follows.

None of this sounds bad—in fact, many of these attributes are critical for any leader, and some types of management roles (and even some types of companies) actually work best under this model. But in terms of influencing, developing, and engaging employees, our research shows that these qualities alone will not get the same results that a Mentor Manager can achieve.

In contrast to the traditional leader, a *Mentor Manager* looks like this:

- They take the time for one-on-one coaching, focusing on professional and personal growth. A mentor helps a person move forward and overcome obstacles.

- They shift the focus to the employee and the employee's professional and personal goals. A mentor helps others establish their paths, values, and purposes—both within the company and outside of it—instead of just focusing on the company's needs or goals.

- They have the ability to focus on the people on the ship, as well as where the ship is headed. A mentor's focus is people-driven instead of entity-driven.

- They stand next to their employees, and walk the path with them.

Take a moment to recall some of the greatest stories you can think of: films, screenplays, books—the format doesn't matter. There might be several reasons why each of these individual stories resonate with you, but there is usually one thing that they have in common: a mentor. Luke had Obi-Wan Kenobi, Katniss had Haymitch, Frodo had Gandalf, Rocky had Mick. What made these characters mentors? It's that they sparked the possibility of what could be. They were the keystones and, often, the missing link that connected their students to their dreams.

When you look at the greatest mentors from film and literature, there are five traits that you'll see appearing again and again: confidence, credibility, competence, candor, and the ability to care. We'll take a deep dive into each of these characteristics in chapter ten, but for now, try to become alert to these five traits and learn to recognize them when you see them. Once you begin to adopt them into your own life and your own way of relating to people, they are what will ultimately qualify you to be a mentor to others. Your employees will recognize that effort, and, in turn, they will put in the effort to connect with you.

The greatest leaders are the ones who can both practice mentorship and teach it. Don't burn yourself out by trying to mentor everybody who walks through your door. You can't become a mentor until your employees invite you into their heart. By being the type of manager your people *want* to connect with, you allow them to become a partner in defining the boundaries of a healthy working relationship.

Assessing Your Own Ways of Leading

Take a moment to evaluate how you lead and connect to your people. What are your strengths? Often we are really good at the development side of our industry and at the development of those who work for us—but how good are we at the connection side of things?

Stephen R. Covey said, "Leadership is communicating to another person their worth and potential so clearly that they are inspired to see it in themselves."[3] As much as I love Covey, I want to offer a slightly different perspective. I agree that the theory behind this saying is nearly spot on, but the Undercover Millennial program has taught me that that there is an underlying complexity to this idea that has a lot to do with mentorship.

A leader is someone who can get others to follow them. There are many good leaders who can do this, but who still fall short in their ability to get people to believe in themselves. That is a key difference between the results of traditional leadership and the results from leadership that is founded on being a mentor. Traditional leaders mostly focus on the destination, while mentors focus on the people and the journey toward the destination. Attributes of traditional leadership and strong mentorship are both necessary, and when you can demonstrate both, that's when you create the greatest opportunity for greater profitability, influence, and loyalty that lasts.

Here's this line of thinking in a nutshell: "Great mentors can communicate someone's potential and worth so clearly that the person begins to recognize that potential and worth in themselves."

That's how I would like you to apply the lessons from this chapter. Never underestimate the power you can have as a Mentor Manager, or your ability to move people, whether that's mentally, physically, or emotionally. The possibilities of your influence are limitless.

Take a moment to evaluate where you land as a Mentor Manager. Honestly ask yourself the following questions (referring to the management styles chart on page 60 as needed):

- If I have been operating as a Removed Manager (low expectations, low connection), why is it that I feel like I can't engage with my employees? Why am I keeping my distance? Why am I reluctant to express high expectations?

- If I have been operating as a Buddy Manager (low expectations, high connection), why is it that I feel like I have to be everyone's friend first, and their boss second? What am I telling myself that prevents me from holding boundaries? What am I afraid I will lose if I show up in what I perceive to be a managerial capacity?

- If I have been operating as a Controlling Manager (high expectations, low connection), where did this come from? Where in my life did I learn that it had to be "my way or the highway"? Where have I experienced this before in my professional life?

- If I have been operating as a Mentor Manager (high expectations, high connection), what are the benefits of my managerial style? How can I continue to improve in being the mentor that my employees need me to be? What is working, and what can I change to improve upon the mentoring process?

We Learn Through Experience and Example

After my airplane hangar experience, I turned to hospitality, working at a resort that had a beautiful warm-water natural crater nestled into the Wasatch Mountains of Utah. It seemed like a great job when I got hired, but I soon viewed my boss

Great mentors can communicate someone's potential and worth so clearly that the person begins to recognize that potential and worth in themselves.

as a tyrant. I don't remember ever hearing an encouraging word. I felt constantly micromanaged and criticized, and my co-workers felt the same. Consequently, none of us worked there for very long. I remained in hospitality after that, but at a different resort, where I had the incredible opportunity to work with an older man we called Lee the Bell Captain.

After leaving his high-paying consultancy business, Lee had come to the Zermatt Resort, a luxury hotel, to work in management. Lee was a smart guy and loved people. When he graduated with a master's degree in audiology and speech therapy, his goal was to become a medical doctor, and he was quickly accepted into a program that involved working at the Mayo Clinic. He spent the summer before the program working with an otolaryngologist and decided to change career directions—he found he wanted to work *with* people, not on them.

So Lee went back to school to become a communicative-disorders specialist, and eventually landed work as a speech therapist for people with disabilities. He had loved that line of work, but eventually retired from it. By the time I met him, Lee was in his third career.

At the time, the only thing I knew about Lee was that this old guy was one of the hardest-working people I had ever met. He arrived every morning with a huge smile on his face and an infectious energy of enthusiasm. While his main responsibility at the resort was to help hire and train the bell staff, he also took fantastic care of the conference presenters and event teams that came into town. He made them look so good! He never worried about recognition. Instead of needing to be noticed, Lee noticed things about other people and was always the first to offer recognition.

Right away, I could tell that Lee was a different type of manager from any I had worked with before. From my very first day, he made me aware of my strengths, and found ways we could capitalize on them. "Clint," he said to me, "when I saw that last car pull up, I was so happy to see how you noticed the elderly woman at the wheel. I saw you run over and open her front door so quickly. And how cautious you were with her—so kind and friendly as you helped her out of the car. Now, that's the type of thing that can really make a difference in another person's life!"

Immediate connection.

Lee made it a pleasure to come to work every day. As he worked with me and the other bellhops, he continuously reinforced our strengths. Whenever we were messing around or made a mistake, he would pull us aside individually and give us advice on how we could do our jobs better. Lee had very high expectations, which he communicated to us by his *example* and then reinforced through his *teaching* and his *training*. Instead of being a team that was focused on tips and money, we focused on our customers and the needs they had. As a byproduct, the tips poured in.

We learned to love people as much as Lee did, and we concentrated on making sure their stay with us was as pleasant as possible. I learned to memorize names and faces, and to take special care of people's belongings and cars. When I did make a mistake, Lee never threatened to fire me, nor did he make me feel less than anyone else. He simply mentored me into a better frame of mind. Every mistake created an opportunity to learn greater things about myself and what was possible in my job.

Lee also knew 90 percent more about me than any manager I had ever had. He cared. He asked me questions about my life, school, girls, my hopes and dreams, and so on. And it wasn't just me—he did this with everybody. Some of the employees were musicians or actors studying theater; Lee

Connection and high standards
need to be placed on equal footing.

attended our concerts and performances, and invited us to break bread together. He cared when someone was ill or struggling. He was a remarkable Mentor Manager, with clearly communicated high expectations and a high connection with each of us.

Even though we didn't know about Lee's past careers, the other bellhops and I knew that Lee was special and could likely do anything in the world.

"Why on earth are you doing this job?" I asked him one day. "You could be getting paid ten times more!"

The only response Lee gave was, "I love my job!"

He proved that sentiment every day by showing us we were more valuable to him than any paycheck could possibly be.

To confirm my memories about Lee, I called the Zermatt Resort last year and spoke with the general manager. Having had the pleasure of working with Lee for nearly a decade, he was happy to share all of the remarkable things that Lee represented. He also conveyed how sad they were when Lee finally retired from Zermatt. Given that the hospitality industry happens to have one of the highest employee turnover rates in the world (losing 60 to 300 percent annually, according to the U.S. Bureau of Labor Statistics[4]), I was mostly curious about Lee's retention rate as a bell captain.

Zermatt's director of human resources confirmed that in the nearly ten years of Lee's management, they needed to hire only forty-nine bellhops—an average of roughly five per year, which is unheard of in that industry.

The remarkable thing about all of this is that when I interviewed Lee about the number of bellhops he had worked with over that ten-year span, he simply said, "A little less than fifty." Do you know how he knew? He remembered every single person he'd ever worked with. He could tell you their names and an impressive bit of information about each one of them.

Lee the Bell Captain taught me to live with passion—he taught me to serve, love, and genuinely care about people. More importantly, he believed in me. He saw many things in me that I had never seen in myself—things like the joy of giving, a love of people, my potential and future as a father, the career choices I had in front of me and where they could take me. When I left Zermatt, I was more equipped to live my own life better. I understood how to serve better and how to work hard in order to succeed in the medical sales industry, which I entered into next. The lessons I learned from Lee (and incorporated into my everyday life) helped me succeed very quickly.

I understand now that Lee was an anomaly in the hospitality industry. Fascinatingly enough, this man went from becoming a doctor to being an educator and then a bell captain, and now (well past retirement age) he has decided to go back to work again—this time at Trader Joe's. On his very first day, management saw the genuine way that Lee handled the customers and immediately asked him to mentor the other staff members. How many people do you know who have been asked to be a Mentor Manager on their very first day? I'm sure it's not many.

I hope that Lee the Bell Captain has helped you see that it's possible for you to be an anomaly in your very own way—a Mentor Manager that is uniquely suited to you.

In business, we have no problem setting goals, quoting numbers, or understanding the value and importance of a mission statement—we do it fairly well because these are generally seen as the biggest priority. But what suffers the most is the connection piece. That's what's missing. Connection and high standards need to be placed on equal footing. In doing so, you create an empowered workforce—and empowered workforces always have greater productivity.

Nearly every employee you will ever have carries an innate desire to become better than who they are. As a Mentor Manager, you'll have the unique opportunity to take that ember that lies inside everyone, and carefully breathe life into it. Through your efforts, you can help each employee recognize what the world has to offer and what they can offer the world. You can encourage them to become not just the best *in* their team, but the best *for* their team—and the best for your business.

MASTERING YOUR MOMENTS

Question #1: Think of a recent experience you had mentoring an employee. What prompted you to mentor them?

Question #2: How did the employee react to your mentorship? Was a connection made?

Question #3: How can you both better communicate clear expectations and establish a greater connection with your employees? How will you build trust as a mentor?

Challenge: Be the mentor you were fortunate enough to have
Think of the great mentors in your life and write down their names. List at least three. What values and traits did these mentors have? What made them so significant in your life? Why did you connect with them?

Now, evaluate your own mentor relationship with your employees. How can you have as much of an impact as these great mentors had in your life? What personal traits can you improve in yourself to have a greater connection with your employees?

Troublemaker, problem child, these were the labels I had allowed to settle into my young heart.

— 5 —

SPARKING
THE POSSIBILITY

**Success isn't just about what you accomplish
in your life. It's about what you inspire others to do.**
TERRY WILDEMANN

HOLDING STILL has never been something that comes
easy for me. When I was in fifth grade, I was teased with
nicknames like "the twitcher" or "the tapper" because
I would always tap on my desk. I couldn't stop moving—
and most of the time I wasn't even aware I was doing it. If
my hands weren't moving, my feet were, and vice versa. The
movement usually happened whenever I was trying to focus
on something, like reading or listening to the teacher. I don't
blame others for getting annoyed with me, because if you've
ever sat next to somebody who is constantly clicking their
pen or tapping their foot, you can relate to the irritation.

On one occasion, a teacher got so frustrated with me for
disrupting the class with my endless tapping that she sent
me to the principal. I had never been to the principal's office
before, and I was very nervous to meet him. Walking down

the hall to his office, I drew out each step, walking as slowly and methodically as possible to postpone the inevitable. Thoughts of punishment raced through my mind. To a kid—at least in my day—the principal's office is like the school's torture chamber. Cities have prisons. Heaven has Hell. And schools have the principal's office.

As I walked through the door of the office, the principal sat waiting for me with a stern face. He seemed just as frightening as I had pictured him.

"What happened?" he said. "Why did your teacher send you to see me?"

I had rehearsed a thousand things to say: "She thought I was such an exceptional student that you should see me in person for an award." That seemed hard to sell. Or maybe: "Our class pet is loose in the building. It may have rabies." I could maybe even escape in the panic.

In the end, I had nothing to say but the truth. "I... I... think it's because... I tap."

The principal looked at me in surprise.

"What?" he exclaimed. "For tapping?" His nose scrunched and he looked at my small frame as if skeptical.

"Yes," I replied. I thought I might have to sell a lie, but not the truth. Why was it so hard to believe that my teacher sent me to the office for tapping? "Half the time I don't even know that I'm doing it," I continued. "I promise I don't mean to do it on purpose. I just can't help it."

"Hmmm," he said with a nod. It was clear he wasn't quite sure what to do with my situation. After a moment of thought, he leaned over his desk and said, "Okay. Here's the deal. I'm going to send you back to class. And when you feel like you need to hit something, I want you to just... sit on your hands."

I thought, "Sit on my hands? Why would I do that?" I was confused.

"All right," I replied. I guess I thought it was a decent request, considering the other torturous punishments I had imagined on the way to his office. He excused me, sending me back to class.

Quietly, I walked back into the classroom, took my seat, and tried to pay attention to the lesson. Less than five minutes later, my right hand started to tap my desk. It only took a few taps before I remembered what the principal had told me. Like an ethereal wise man speaking from beyond the ages, my principal's voice sounded in my head: "Clint, sit on your hands."

Sheepishly, I glanced around the room. Sitting on my hands was about the most absurd thing I could think of doing, but, then again, many things adults said seemed absurd to me at that age. I took a last glance around to make sure no one was watching and scooted my hands under my seat. Despite the discomfort of having my palms wedged under my rump, I tried with all my might to concentrate on the lesson. But the stillness didn't last long; as soon as I stopped thinking about my hands, my feet began tapping rapidly on the floor.

I let out a noticeable sigh of frustration as I threw my head back. How was I supposed to sit on my feet? I was a lost cause.

That same year, I had another teacher, by the name of Mr. Jensen. He was an older English teacher who had been in the education world for a very long time. He had snow-white hair, he wore big Coke-bottle glasses that teetered on his nose, sometimes he wore suspenders, and he always wore a red tie.

During one of my tapping episodes in his class, he stopped the lesson and scanned the classroom. When his gaze settled on me, his thick glasses magnified the intensity of his stare.

"Clint Pulver," he said sternly. The eyes of every student in the class immediately fixed on me. I slid down in my chair and tried to shrink into my desk, but it was just not big enough. "Is that you tapping?"

Even at that young age, I knew this was what adults liked to call a rhetorical question. He knew it was me. Everyone knew it was me. I'm sure at some point there was a city newsletter with the headline: CLINT TAPS LOUDLY IN CLASS.

I nodded my head in defeated acknowledgment. I was as annoyed with my body as everyone else was annoyed with me. I just couldn't help it.

"I want you to stay after class to talk," he said. The faces of my classmates turned from disapproval into that wide-eyed gaze I imagine people give to a person condemned to the gallows.

Fear and anxiety leapt into my heart. I had been yelled at all year by just about every teacher in the school and had already been sent to the principal's office. Even bullies weighed in on their dislike for my tapping. And now Mr. Jensen. What was *he* going to do to me?

The class bell rang and everyone was dismissed. The clamor of gathering books and chatter erupted around me as the students filed excitedly out of class. After a few long minutes, the cacophony settled into a deathly silence. Still, I remained in my chair. The classroom was empty, except for me and Mr. Jensen.

He looked at me for a long while. His face showed no harshness or disappointment, the usual expressions adults had when talking to me about my tapping. He pulled a chair up to his desk until it was right next to him and motioned to it, inviting me for a chat.

"Do you know why I told you to stay after class?" he asked.

"Yes," I replied. "It's because I tap."

"You've become quite the talk of the school," he said, amused. "They say you're a troublemaker. At least, that's what the teachers say."

I remained silent, directing my attention to my feet, which had already begun to wiggle. I couldn't deny the accusations.

At the time, that's the only way I knew how to describe myself. Troublemaker, problem child, these were the labels I had allowed to settle into my young heart.

"They tell me you can't sit still in class," he continued. "You fidget."

"I'm sorry, Mr. Jensen," I pleaded. "I don't mean to. Honest. It's just..."

Mr. Jensen cut me off, "Clint, I've been watching you," he said. "I watch what you do in my class every time you try to focus on what's being taught. Your right hand starts to move..." Mr. Jensen raised his right hand and began wiggling it. He then raised his left hand and began wiggling that. "And then your left hand will start to move at a totally different tempo." He grinned as he placed his hands back down. I smiled too.

"You know what that's called in big adult words?" he asked.

I shook my head.

"Ambidextrous."

I had never heard that word before and had no clue what he was talking about. It sounded like some strange alien disease out of a science fiction book.

He recognized my confusion and said, "Here—I'll show you what I mean. Can you tap your head and rub your belly at the same time? Try it."

I gave it a go. I began tapping my head with one hand, then followed up with my other hand, rubbing lightly on my belly. It was no problem at all.

"Now switch the rhythm of your hands," said Mr. Jensen. I did just as he said—still no problem. "Now tap your belly and rub your head."

It took a little more concentration that time, but, sure enough, I could do it.

"Now switch back. Great!" he said. "Now switch again. Again."

Back and forth I went, shifting between alternating patterns. My right and left limbs were working totally independently of each other, with little or no effort on my part.

Mr. Jensen leaned back in his chair and gave a slight chuckle, as if to say to himself, "I knew it!"

"Clint," he said, "I don't think you're a problem. I think you're a drummer." He then opened the top drawer of his desk and reached inside, pulling out a pair of drumsticks. He carefully handed them to me.

With uncertainty, I took them from Mr. Jensen. I'll be honest—as a ten-year-old boy, I didn't realize the significance of what was happening, or how this seemingly simple act would change the course of my life.

When Mr. Jensen gave me those drumsticks, they came with one condition. "Clint, these drumsticks are for you," he said. "I want you to have them. But I also want you to promise me one thing."

"What?" I asked. Distracted by the novelty of having my own drumsticks, I couldn't take my eyes off them.

"Promise me that you'll try to keep them in your hands as much as possible. When you feel like you have a lot of energy or that you have to move, pick up your sticks and start playing. Just keep them in your hands and let's see what happens."

"Okay!" I exclaimed with delight.

That moment was more than twenty-two years ago, and I have tried to keep my promise to Mr. Jensen every day since. I've had the opportunity to tour and record all over the world as a professional drummer, and I've appeared on shows like *America's Got Talent*. I started the first drumline at my high school and then went on to college, at the largest university in Utah, to start its first drumline, called the Green Man Group. It exists to this day, helping to provide the highest-paying scholarships for drummers at the collegiate level.

It's not about being
the best *in* the world—
**it's about being
the best *for* the world.**

After college, I coached the drumline for the Jazz NBA team for four years before moving on to new adventures.

With the help of this talent, I was honored to graduate with my bachelor's degree from Utah Valley University with zero college debt. Music scholarships and other performance drumming opportunities helped pay for my college education. I don't tell you this to boast about how cool I am or to gain recognition. I share these things with you to show you the impact that just one person had in my life. It was another one of those single moments in time that made my life a better story. Mr. Jensen was the first person who looked at what most people saw as a problem and turned it into an opportunity. He allowed me to see something within myself that I might not otherwise have ever seen.

Like Sir Isaac Newton pointed out, "If I have seen further, it is by standing upon the shoulders of giants." I was able to see further down the road of my life and potential only because Mr. Jensen had a gigantic heart and allowed me to stand on his shoulders. Your employees need you to do the same for them. Let them stand on your shoulders, or at least give them a leg up, so that they can see further down their own path and begin to recognize the greatness within them.

Let it be known that I am not the best drummer in the world. There are plenty who are faster, are more advanced, or have flawless technique. I've said it before and I'll say it again now, because *this* is the main lesson from this story: it's not about being the best *in* the world... it's about being the best *for* the world.

Was Mr. Jensen the best fifth-grade teacher in the world? Who knows? Who cares? Did he worry about whether he was the best teacher when deciding to give me drumsticks? I'm sure he did not. What he did do was teach me about the power of being the best *for* others, and he did this through his service, his giving, and his advocacy. He didn't give me drumsticks so he could be voted teacher of the year or receive recognition or praise. He did it because he wanted the best for me. He evaluated what he could do and offer, and he didn't hold back, thinking his action was too small to have an effect. I didn't know it at the time, but he provided me with one of the best examples of servant leadership I've ever witnessed, and he showed me what can happen when you choose to be the best for your people.

Two things that Mr. Jensen did that day are the same two things I see today in my undercover research—things that work miracles in terms of building lasting loyalty in the workplace. Mr. Jensen communicated my worth, and he communicated my potential. And he did it so well that I began to see both of those things within myself. If you can communicate these same two things to your employees, you will make a world of difference in the way they engage and work.

We don't always have a clear understanding of what's in front of us or what lies within ourselves—until, that is, someone changes our perception. Once our perception is changed, the way we view and internalize information also changes. Our reality begins to shift, and our behavior follows suit. You have the opportunity to change the perception and shift the reality of the people who work with you and for you. You can be someone's Mr. Jensen.

If you think of *worth* and *potential* as two locked boxes that sit inside each person, what then are the keys? Helping someone recognize their own worth takes recognition. And allowing someone to realize their potential requires giving them lots of opportunities for growth.

WORTH → RECOGNITION

POTENTIAL → GROWTH OPPORTUNITIES

You can remind an employee of their worth simply by recognizing them for a job well done. Or, like Mr. Jensen did, you can go further and show them recognition on a deeper level: *I see you*. Likewise, you can help your employees see their own potential—and help them reach it—by giving them opportunities to take on new challenges and expand their skill set.

Without recognition and opportunities for growth, your employees' ability to find worth in their work and see their potential for success is greatly dampened. As their Mentor Manager, you are responsible for creating an environment where these qualities can be encouraged and fostered.

But how do you do it? Where do you even start? Potential is a tricky beast, and much of this book is about finding, nurturing, and mentoring that potential. We talked about potential in the previous chapter, and we'll get into it even more deeply in chapters seven, eight, and eleven. Recognition, however, can be surprisingly simple. So let's break that one down right now.

Creating a Culture of Recognition

Everybody needs to feel important and worthwhile—and communicating to employees what you see in them allows them to feel that worth in themselves. During all my years undercover, I have kept track of the "I love it here" responses and the culture that surrounds them, and I've found that recognition is a huge factor in the satisfaction of employees. Of course, small businesses differ from large, and the same methods of expressing recognition that work well in one organization are not always a huge success in another, but across those cultures, I often see very similar ways of offering recognition come up. Let's have a look at some of the most common, and most successful.

Offer vocal praise. Words of affirmation are something we need and yearn for from day one. From a very young age, we receive encouragement and praise as we learn to crawl, walk, talk, do our chores, score well on tests, get into colleges, or get new jobs. It's not needy; it's how we know we're on the right track. "Brandon," an employee at an online marketing company, told me that the most defining moment he experienced at work was when the manager spent half of a company meeting simply going around, employee to employee, and sharing a list of the unique contributions to growing the business that each individual had made during the holiday season. Many of the insights the manager shared focused on the goodness of that individual and who they were as a person. This vocal praise meant more to the employee than any free food or celebratory event. It was what the employees I spoke to cherished the most, and the cool thing is that this big deposit of trust and loyalty cost that manager nothing but a bit of time.

Provide experiences. We live in a place and time—especially in terms of the younger generations—where phrases like YOLO (you only live once) and "do it for the Insta!" are beloved mantras. People love to post updates on what they're doing, where they are, and what they plan to do later. Younger generations today tend to treasure experiences over things, which makes gift certificates and event tickets excellent forms of recognition. Think skydiving, scuba diving, surf lessons, ax throwing, ziplining, massages, concerts, theater, art exhibitions, sporting events—just make sure you tailor the experience to the individual. (You don't want someone to be strapping on a parachute and thinking, "Really? You couldn't

just get tickets to *Hamilton*?") If you're of an older generation that's used to more tangible—think: *investable*—rewards,
gifts like these may seem strange, or a little pointless. But
trust me: give your employees unforgettable experiences, and
they'll share them with their friends on newsfeeds and blog
entries for months to come. That's recruitment buzz that
can't be bought.

Give them freedom. Many companies we've visited give their
employees unlimited days off as long as their work gets done
well and on time. This is an emerging and powerful trend
in the workplace—people can come and go as they need to,
taking it on their own initiative to make sure they're meeting
the standards set for their role. For employers, it's not about
time off; it's about quality time on. This autonomy sends a
message of trust to the employees and drives them to use
their time productively rather than just waiting out the hours.
And you don't even have to go that far. Allow employees to
work from home, come in after hours, come in early in the
morning. Give employees recognition through the freedom
to define the schedule that works for them, and the trust you
show by allowing them to make their own choices. Some people might have reservations about giving such discretion to
their employees. What if they abuse the system? Hiring the
right people in the first place will help alleviate the fear of
being taken advantage of.

Provide food. You may think this perk is extravagant or
unnecessary, but there are more benefits to it than you may
realize. Providing food for your employees can actually be
cost effective, saving time and energy your people need to
step out of the workplace to grab their lunch or afternoon
coffee. More than that, free food is also effective in just about
any quantity. Are you able to provide lunches for your people?

Great! Does that seem too much? What about a weekly tradition of "cupcake Fridays" or tacos on Tuesday? Special days like these can not only help your people keep their energy and spirits up, they also give them a chance to mingle and connect—like the donuts that helped bring a manager's team together in chapter three. Evaluate what you can do. A little food can go a long way. Food: 5 stars—highly recommended.

Reward them with money. Obviously, extra cash in the form of a raise or a bonus is always a welcome reward and a great form of recognition. Salary increases, gift cards—anything extra, really. We've seen that giving a monetary reward not only offers recognition, it also shows good will and puts the company in a good light. Your employees will be more willing to work for you—and more likely to enjoy that work—when you invest your money back into them. It's important to emphasize here that many believe the younger generations prioritize money less than older generations might—that purpose always outweighs wealth. While this may be true, you also have to remember that, yes, they still value money! If you've been told that millennials or Gen Z don't care about money, you need to know that this is simply not the case. Here's my two cents, based on many years of interviews and research: money, as recognition, will always be well received.

Offer fun toys and gifts. Think Christmas, think birthdays, think presents. I don't care who you are or what you do or don't believe in (Santa is real!)—everyone loves a thoughtful gift. Everyone loves to have something to open. A GoPro, tech gadgets, AirPods, athletic wear, a watch, a book—gifts like these offered to show recognition and appreciation will bring moments of joy to the lives of your employees, moments they'll remember for a long time. But! Be smart. Be appropriate. Be professional. Don't use this advice as a free

Recognition and gifts *must* be **personalized as much as possible.**

pass to give inappropriate items to employees that cross the line of respect, whether that's in relation to gender, religious belief, personal boundaries, or anything else. Also, while company swag—hats, shirts, gym bags, sports bottles, and so on—can be a great (and potentially more affordable) option for small, in-the-moment rewards, keep the logo and design simple, and make sure you get the best quality and utility you can afford. A cheap, impractical, or uncomfortable item that the employee would not be proud to wear or use in public is more of a burden than a gift.

Award them. Giving an award is about visibility. Display the employee's name on something tangible, whether that's a plaque, a trophy, or a medal. Think along the lines of a Grammy: something that's worth putting on the mantel and has some sort of value. The key word there is *value*. If you give a printout of a certificate as a reward for a project that took months and landed a major client, that could seem insulting and have the reverse effect from what you want to achieve. Also, consider mentioning the employee in the company newsletter, or on some digital platform where all their colleagues can see it. Now you've given them a concrete accomplishment that can raise their profile in the company.

These forms of recognition don't necessarily need to come from the highest executives. In fact, there's nothing like peer-to-peer respect and recognition, whether that's a direct nomination or an inter-company vote. You can even hold a company event like an awards night and invite your employees' family members and close friends. By doing this, you encourage your whole team to pay attention to the achievements of those around them. That keeps everybody in the organization looking for the good in others, and focuses on what's right, instead of what's wrong.

Whichever method you choose, the most important thing to remember is to try your best to customize that recognition to each individual. This is an excellent opportunity to show that you listen and care. A reward that is personalized to the interests of the individual sends the message that they are seen not as a cog in the machinery of the company but as a person with a unique life of their own.

As you get to know your employees, listen carefully when they talk about what they do with their time away from work, and don't be afraid to ask them about the things they love and enjoy. What are their hobbies? Do they love to cook or bake? Are they master gardeners or woodworkers? Avid DIYers? Do they bike, hike, camp, ski? Do they travel every chance they get, or are they homebodies? Are they building their family nest, or getting ready to downsize and simplify their lives?

Everybody receives recognition differently, so I can't emphasize this enough: recognition and gifts *must* be personalized as much as possible. And asking each employee directly how they would prefer to be recognized is a surefire way to provide each with the unique recognition they value most. Those are the two things I would like you to take away from this topic: when giving recognition, *ask* and *personalize*.

At the risk of stating the obvious, remember also that awards and recognition should be given only for a job well done. Focus on your employees' progress, character growth, and accomplishments, while telling them *why* they're receiving their reward. Whether it's a salary increase, an experience, a gift card, a pat on the back, or simply a thank-you card, make sure that every type of recognition is followed with the reason they're receiving it. This lets them know they're being noticed—and, more importantly, being *seen* for the value they bring.

Acknowledging the Need for Growth

As I said before, providing your employees with opportunities for growth is an ongoing process, and needs to be woven in to every aspect of your leadership—from choosing your team to developing relationships to mentoring and promoting from within, right down to examining and refining your own management style. But there are also a few day-to-day steps you can take to make it clear to your employees that their growth is important to you. In our research, we have seen a lot of great results come from managers who provided these four types of growth opportunities:

1 Call out their potential.
2 Make simple investments.
3 Arrange trainings, speakers, and workshops.
4 Offer your advocacy.

Let's dig down a bit into each of these, so you can see how you could incorporate them into your everyday work culture. Ensuring plenty of small moments like these can help establish trust in your employees that you are looking out for their future.

1. Call out their potential

Sometimes, it's as small as creating a moment where you can tell one of your team members about the opportunities you see them growing into—such as becoming a future leader, moving into management, or any other career move that may excite and motivate them. This also gives you the chance to talk about their performance, their strengths and abilities, and the benefits that these could bring to the future of the organization, and to their own future as well.

Think back to the previous chapter, and how Lee the Bell Captain pulled me aside to tell me how the way I was connecting with customers showed a lot of potential for my future. It meant a lot to me, and I will always remember it. In our undercover research, the employees we speak with also talk often about the moments when they have been seen for the good and potential they possess. Look for that good yourself, and don't forget to call it out.

2. Make simple investments

Investing in your employees' development as individuals as well as professionals can yield very positive results—these authentic conversations can reveal not just where an employee wants to go, but also who they want to be. From there, one simple and effective step you can take is to offer them a book. That's right—just a book! I once interviewed an employee whose manager gave everyone their own new book about personal development every year, each chosen specially to match a specific employee's personal or professional goals (goals that the manager had gleaned from conversations held throughout the year).

This employee absolutely cherished those books. They were also meaningful to the manager, who had read them beforehand in order to better understand the people and to ensure the book would be worth the employee's time. Certainly not everyone will appreciate a book, and not every manager has the time to read dozens. But the point is to learn how to invest in your employees' development in ways that suit them.

It so happens that books *are* my thing, so here's a list of some of my personal favorites that I've seen used this way in my interviews and research:

- *The War of Art* by Steven Pressfield
- *You Don't Need a Title to Be a Leader* by Mark Sanborn
- *Daring Greatly* by Brené Brown
- *A Million Miles in a Thousand Years* by Donald Miller
- *Cure for the Common Life* by Max Lucado
- *Start with Why* by Simon Sinek
- *You Are a Badass* by Jen Sincero
- *Nice Bike* by Mark Scharenbroich
- *How to Win Friends and Influence People* by Dale Carnegie
- *Man's Search for Meaning* by Viktor Frankl
- *The Courage to Be Rich* by Suze Orman
- *Good to Great* by Jim Collins
- *As a Man Thinketh* by James Allen
- *The Work of This Moment* by Toni Packer
- *When Things Fall Apart* by Pema Chödrön
- *Walking on Water* by Madeleine L'Engle

3. Arrange trainings, speakers, and workshops

If you've ever seen a great speaker nail it in a TED talk, conference, or church meeting, you know how effective they can be at inspiring and motivating people. A good motivational speaker can help remind your employees of what they do and why they do it—and hearing the message that you've been trying to convey from someone new can sometimes deliver it in a fresh way. Make sure the speaker is the right fit and has some credibility, and involve your team when you're choosing topics or guests.

Sending your employees to workshops, courses, or even professional development conferences—even if they're online—also shows your team that you're willing to invest in their careers and their lives. What skills or technologies do they want to learn? Do they need to keep up with programming languages, web tech?

I've seen many companies that offer life skills training (such as negotiation, parenting, stress management, home finances, and so on). On the other side of that coin, I've seen others who promote their people into management based on seniority (which is great for internal hires), but offer zero training to help them grow into their new responsibilities. It's like standing in front of a fireplace and saying, "Give me heat, then I'll give you wood." It doesn't work that way.

If you want to develop future leaders, give them ways to build their skills in communication, motivation, trust, finance management, teamwork, goal setting, achievement, customer service, crucial conversations and conflict resolution, accountability, delegation, strategy, creativity, and (of course) leadership. Fernanda Böhme, CEO and co-founder of Böhme, a clothing chain spread throughout the western U.S., told me that one of her main goals is to make sure her people know there is opportunity for growth if they want it.

"We always tell our people: 'You make your own future,'" she said. "'Böhme is not going to hinder you. If you have the potential, we're going to put you where you're going to grow.'" And Fernanda practices what she preaches. At their corporate office, Böhme offers workshops that specialize in various aspects of the company—window display, graphic design—and they allow any employee who has interest to come and learn exactly what it takes to get to where they

Great mentors know how to **connect people to their dreams**.

want to be. Their efforts to help their employees grow are obviously working—Böhme has been named one of the Top Women-Run Businesses on the *Inc.* 500 Fastest-Growing Companies list, and has been featured in the *Wall Street Journal*, *Forbes*, *Us Weekly*, and *Cosmopolitan*, while also being consistently voted one of the *Salt Lake Tribune*'s Top Workplaces by its employees.

4. Offer your advocacy

Sparking possibility is about learning to advocate for your people, not just develop them. Great mentors know how to connect people to their dreams. In business, we are really good at developing people, but we sometimes fall short in our advocating for them. This is a great loss, because as I experienced myself with Mr. Jensen when he gave me those drumsticks and made me promise to start practicing with them, that kind of advocacy is where the magic happens.

Advocating versus *developing* is a difficult idea to tackle, because they're both equally important. The degree of difference is slight, but the end result is monumental.

My mom was an amazing developer in my life, and still is. I learned many valuable skills and habits because of the way she taught me. When I was twelve years old, I really wanted a full drum set. I approached my mom and told her of my desire.

"I've been working really hard," I said. "I've been studying my best, practicing a lot... I really want to get a drum set."

My mom looked at me and said, "All right. But have you seen your report card recently?"

My head hung low and my shoulders drooped as I let out a sigh. I knew my report card was lacking.

My mother gently placed her hand on my shoulder. "I'll tell you what," she said. "When you change those Cs and Ds to As and Bs, we'll help you get a drum set." From there, she continued to support my academic growth by encouraging me to study, answering my questions, helping me set aside time to complete my work, and maintaining that standard and those clear expectations she had set.

Development. She worked hard to get me to where we both had agreed we wanted me to be. It's important, right?

On the other hand, my dad was an amazing advocate. While I was having this initial conversation with my mom, my dad was sitting in the computer room across the hall. As I walked by the doorway, he leaned over in his chair and whispered, "Clint. *Psst*. Clint, come here."

Confused, I walked to my father's side. He drew in close and said, "Listen. I heard you talking to your mother."

"Yeah. I want a drum set I can play," I replied. "And I've been working really hard."

My dad got up from his chair and walked over to the bottom shelf of his bookcase, where he kept all of his old CDs and records. He pulled out a CD by the prog-rock band Rush. Handing it to me, he pointed to one of the guys on the cover and said, "This guy, this drummer, his name is Neil Peart. And he will change your life. Take a listen. Listen to it, learn it."

I nodded distractedly as I walked away, examining the case in my hands.

"Oh! Wait, wait!" exclaimed my father. He reached up to the second shelf and pulled out another CD, this one by Def Leppard. Pointing to the picture of another musician, he said, "Clint, look at this drummer. This cat doesn't have two arms. He's only got one arm and he plays the drums. If you learn how to play 'Pour Some Sugar on Me,' I'll love you forever."

At first I was equally as impressed that a cat could play the drums as I was by the fact that the cat had one arm, but I did eventually figure out the slang. I learned a lot from my dad, but more than that, he was always advocating.

Can you spot the difference between advocating and developing? I can't stress enough that both are essential to growth. My mom was developing my skills and helping me grow as a person, while my dad realized that I had a dream and showed me the possibilities—he advocated to me, and for me.

Remember Pam Jarvis from chapter three? She once shared with me a story that stands as another great example of this kind of advocacy. One of her medical assistants was having a difficult time working well with the rest of the staff. She struggled to talk to people, was always negative, and had a nasty attitude about everything. One day, Pam overheard her nurse trainer, "Heather," discussing the need to delegate out some of the training to those who excelled in those areas. This struggling M.A. was one of the best at spirometry (a way to test for asthma) in the clinic, and Pam immediately requested that Heather place her in charge of teaching that skill to the entire staff. Here's how it went down:

> She didn't want her to do it, and claimed she was the worst M.A. that we had. But I told her to trust me. So she went to this M.A. and asked her if she would teach, because she was one of the best ones at it, and could really help the training process. And do you know what happened? She comes to work smiling. She talks to people. People invite her to lunch. And I keep getting all these positive feedback comments about how this M.A. has really come into her own. It boosted her confidence. And you know what? We didn't do anything other than give her an opportunity to share what she was really good at.

I think my favorite part of this story is when Pam pointed out that all she did was give the person a chance to utilize her strengths—she had sparked the possibility for this M.A. by communicating her worth and her potential, and then advocating for her to have the opportunity to shine. It's about building people, not just an organization.

Every one of your employees is thinking, "Let me know when it gets to the part about me." Providing these moments in which you show someone their *potential* and their *worth* is not about fulfilling some sense of entitlement—it's just good business. It's about bringing humanity back into the workplace, and becoming the kind of manager who helps people like themselves best when they're working with you.

Great mentors connect people to their dreams.

MASTERING YOUR MOMENTS

Question #1: How can you help shape each employee's perception of themselves and encourage them to see their potential?

Question #2: What can you do to invest in your employees' development, both individually and collectively?

Question #3: What are some programs you can put into place for better employee recognition and growth development?

Challenge: Explore your employees' potential

Make a list that includes everyone on your team, and make notes on where they could grow in the company and the steps they would need to take to get there. List their strengths and other characteristics that you think could help them thrive. In your interactions with your employees, communicate to them where you can imagine them going so that they know you see them in the future of your company.

If you're facing
in the right direction,
**all you have to do
is keep walking**.

KEEP IT SIMPLE

In character, in manners, in style, in all
things, the supreme excellence is simplicity.
HENRY WADSWORTH LONGFELLOW

O F ALL of the practices I have seen implemented by exceptional bosses, one of the greatest is a consistent effort to keep things simple. And this effort extended to every aspect of their oversight: business model, mission statement, even down to their personal life. The art of simplicity has been a major key to their success and their overall ability to lead, and it's had a huge impact on the lives of their employees. The people we interview at these companies who say they love their jobs always mention the simplicity of the culture, the leadership, the direction of the organization, and their job responsibilities.

The Power of Simple Values

If you're facing in the right direction, all you have to do is keep walking. Unfortunately, one of the biggest problems in business is that most employees have no idea which direction

the company is facing—let alone which way they are facing within that company. Many organizations have mission
statements or lists of core values, but the majority of their
employees have no idea what they are. I have given a lot of
keynote addresses, and in them I often pose this question to
the managers and CEOs in attendance: "If you were to hand
out three-by-five cards and ask your employees to explain the
vision of the company, 1) would your employees be able to
provide an answer, and 2) would it be accurate?"

In our research, most employees have been either confused, uninspired, or kept a "this too shall pass attitude"
when it came to the vision of the company. Roughly 87 percent have not been able recite their company's core values,
mission statement, or purpose. Most of the responses sound
like this: "Um... I'm not sure." Or: "I can't really remember.
I know it's something, though!" Once in a while, we'll hear:
"I dunno... 'Do the work and don't get fired'?"

When we kept hearing these same answers, we knew we
had uncovered a systemic problem. But it was in the other
share of employees where we found the solution. We began
to zero in on that 13 percent who did know what their organization stood for and why. Not surprisingly, those employees
were generally the ones who were also much more positive
about their working experiences.

Every organization knows the importance of having a mission statement—or shared goals, core values, or however you
want to refer to it—to know what it is, and how the company
can preserve it as it moves forward. A mission statement is
key to providing purpose, not only for the company, but for
the employees who drive it. Those employees who had inter-
nalized their companies' mission statement and core values
were able to do so because the leaders of their companies
kept those items simple—yet *memorable*. That's all it took.

One of the best companies I have personally witnessed accomplish this is Weave, an emerging tech company that has created a powerful and unique platform to improve scheduling, customer response, online reputation, team workflow, and revenue generation for various organizations. And even though Weave is wildly successful and has had an incredible growth rate (more than 100 percent in their third year!), their focus is their people. Because of this, they have had zero turnover in their product and engineering team in the past two years.

I had the opportunity to meet with Brandon Rodman, one of the co-founders of Weave, and discuss what it was that was driving his company's success. He shared that, when they first started their company, they had developed a mission statement that was so long and intricate that nobody could ever remember it. Sure, it looked great on a wall or on a plaque somewhere, but its purpose was not seen. So they simplified it—a lot—and made it memorable. They cut everything down to three core values:

"Our people are hungry, creative, and caring."

It was simple enough—but Weave knew that they had to make it memorable and observable as well. So they gave every core value a mascot: hungry was represented by a bear, creative was represented by a gorilla, and caring was represented by a sloth. It was one of the best ways I've seen an organization *keep the main thing the main thing*. If you were to casually walk through the office building at Weave's headquarters, you would see phrases and sayings that are all accompanied by bears, gorillas, or sloths—pictures, stuffed animals, and so on. If you were to ask any employee at Weave what their core values are, every single one could answer that question for you. Because they know their company's core values, they know which direction their company is pointing in—creating a movement of company and cultural unity. Simple, yet massively effective.

At Weave, every division in the company, from sales to software development, has a small subset of initiatives that support those three core values. This allows each department to apply the values in a way that fits with their specific duties and roles. "Every time we make a decision as a company, we explain why we are doing it and how it aligns with the three core values," said Brandon. "Everything we live and breathe here at Weave must be centered on those principles."

For example, in 2019, the company's employees competed to collect packaged food, and donated over 24,753 pounds to the local food bank during the Christmas holiday season. They did this to highlight the value "caring" by helping reach and support those in need. Another employee told us about how his son had severe medical issues and how he needed time away from the office to support his family. When the employee returned after his extended time off, an envelope was on his desk with $450 cash donated by his co-workers in the sales department. According to Brandon, caring is practiced at Weave every day. "The organization is always looking for opportunities to reach and support those within our company, as well as those outside of it," he told me.

On the "creative" side of things, Weave has given complete autonomy and freedom to their people so that they feel safe creating and contributing their ideas. On one of the largest walls in the office, there's a quote from the legendary general George Patton: "Don't tell people how to do things. Tell them what to do and let them surprise you with their results." According to Brandon, everybody is allowed to create at Weave, and no idea is left unheard.

Take one of the most impactful and influential ideas that the company has had, which came from an entry-level support employee named "Jessica." When Weave first began as a medical software company, they started out targeting single practices and locations to adopt and buy their software. But because of the creative freedom they gave their employees, Jessica—who was then a customer support worker in the call center—felt empowered to bring forward the idea of creating a whole new marketing approach to target multi-location groups instead of just single offices.

Jessica's creative strategy helped double Weave's revenue and drive its expansion. She was immediately promoted to the role of multi-locations specialist for the whole company, and she continues to innovate and grow her department.

Weave's "hungry" value is heavily emphasized in the hiring and promoting of their managers. The company strives to create a culture of growth and excellence within the leaders, so that they are just as hungry as the people they lead. One manager told us about the energy he experienced on the first day he joined the company. He watched every employee pulling at the same time toward a common goal, the way they communicated with each other, the way they accomplished their work, and the way they helped and assisted other team members when needed. He realized that Weave's culture empowers everybody to elevate their performance for two reasons: that's what's expected, and that's what's being practiced and displayed every single day.

One manager I interviewed, "Jace," said that it was his leadership goal to coach Weave's people into this hungry mentality. But if it wasn't a good fit, he said, it was also his job to "coach them out" and find them a better-suited position that plays to their strengths (within the company, or, occasionally, out of the company). According to Jace, staying hungry required constant support from every co-worker *and* from the leadership team to maintain consistent growth and relevance in the ever-changing world of technology.

Along with simplicity and keeping the vision memorable, a mission statement has to have a sense of realism and authenticity. Does it mean something to your employees, and does it represent them? Does it represent the soul and culture of your organization? When your employees read it, are they proud to be linked with it? Does it inspire them to be a part of something bigger than themselves?

Simplifying Your Schedule

The second major area of simplicity that we've seen contribute to the success of companies and their people is the simplicity of leadership's lives and schedules.

Consider this thought from executive coach Wayne Muller:[1]

> The busier we are, the more important we seem to ourselves and, we imagine, to others. To be unavailable to our friends and family, to be unable to find time for the sunset... to whiz through our obligations without time for a single mindful breath, this has become the model of a successful life.

So often, we find ourselves packing our schedules, filling our days with back-to-back meetings, phone calls, lunches, more meetings, and so on. We worry what perception we will convey by simply sitting in our offices, seemingly doing nothing. *I* know you're not doing nothing, and *you* know you're not doing nothing, but are you afraid that others will think you're doing nothing?

Jeff Civillico, a former headlining performer at the Paris Hotel in Las Vegas and a dear friend of mine, travels the globe as one of the world's premier entertainers and jugglers. One evening we had a conversation about the art of juggling and the elements required to be a great entertainer. I asked him, "What's the world record for the most balls juggled by a juggler?"

He scoffed. "I don't know. It's always changing."

"Okay, okay... but what's the most you've juggled?"

Jeff thought for a moment. "I don't even know if I know that. It's up there, though."

I nodded eagerly. "So we're talking seven, maybe eight?"

He laughed at my enthusiasm. "I've done a lot of things with a lot of juggling balls in my day. But in my show I only do five."

"Only five?" Not as high as I had expected, but still impressive.

"You know why I juggle five balls instead of seven?" he asked.

I knew Jeff was one of the best jugglers around and could likely juggle more than five. Why not put on the big show, juggling seven, nine, or even twelve balls in his show? I shrugged, unable to think of a reason.

Leaning in as if to disclose a trade secret, he said, "The audience doesn't remember how many balls you juggled. What they *do* remember is how many balls you dropped."

That idea has stuck with me. It may be more impressive to juggle more balls, but by juggling fewer, you increase your success rate. Does that mean we should shoot for lower goals and keep to what's safe? Absolutely not. Jeff doesn't shy away from the hard stuff; he once *joggled* (jogging while juggling) the entire Disney Marathon, 26.2 miles, for charity. He's no stranger to tackling hard things, and he incorporates some amazing feats into his show. But only when it counts. The rest of the time, he keeps it simple and sticks to what he does best.

How does this principle apply to your management? I want you to ask yourself two questions:

- When I come into work, how do my employees experience me?

- How do they experience themselves when they are with me?

If you're consumed with your business, your life, your job, your office duties, and so on, then that tired, burned-out persona will become the core message you convey to your staff.

We've found through our undercover work that the leaders who have the highest employee regard are the ones who are masters at keeping things simple—not only within their leadership, but also throughout their businesses. This simplicity allows for better interaction with employees and greater access to them as leaders. For the most part, it comes down to priorities, and being great at creating boundaries and standards that lend themselves to simplicity. I call it the power of their "to don't" list. Instead of creating a "to do" list like many of us do, they have often been intentional about clarifying the things they won't do with their time on a given day, or even as a standing rule.

A "to don't" list like this might include things like "no emails after 5 p.m.," or "leave work at work," or "put my cellphone in a drawer when I'm meeting with an employee." One employee at a tire franchise we visited praised how their boss had an open-door hour every day from 3 p.m. to 4 p.m., where they would completely dedicate their attention to meeting with employees, allowing them the freedom to come and go from their office whenever they needed.

Whatever you're doing and whomever you're doing it with deserves the gift of your time and attention. An inaccessible leader is of no benefit to a team. Do your employees feel free to speak to you whenever they need? Can they get ahold of you during the workday? We've found that the best

An inaccessible leader is of **no benefit to a team**.

Mentor Managers have open-door policies. Employees have the freedom to come and check in, ask a question, make a suggestion, or say hello, similar to that manager at the tire franchise. Certainly there are boundaries to this: employees or colleagues are not entitled to know about every meeting or interrupt whenever they please. But if your staff has access to your basic schedule and knows when you'll be available, they'll have a greater sense of security.

So many of the employees I interview are just looking for a little bit of time from their boss. Are you allowing that to happen? Employees spell mentorship with T-I-M-E. By creating simplicity in their lives, leaders create the time and ability to invest in their people with greater dedication, empathy, love, and connection.

What Can You Stop Doing?

One way to simplify your schedule and make time for people is to stop doing activities that you don't love doing or that aren't advancing your goals. It's really as simple as that: stop doing things that aren't helping you. Now, your brain might be throwing up red flags all over the place: "I can't do that!" and "It's not that easy" and "I don't quit" and "Quitting doesn't get you where you want to go!" You've probably seen at least one of these famous quotes, which are always floating around the internet in different variations and with wide-ranging attributions:

"Quitters never win and winners never quit."

"Successful people keep moving."

"If you quit once, it becomes a habit."

"Quitting is the easiest thing to do."

While inspirational on the surface, these messages can actually be profoundly deceiving. The truth is, people quit things all the time. And you should too. Who are the people that you need to take a break from? What are the time-consuming tasks you can stop doing, allowing you more time to give to other things? What habits do you have that need to be re-thought? What can you learn to say no to?

The difference lies in *what* you quit, as great leaders and successful Mentor Managers know. But we hesitate to make the change, because we worry that we don't know how to quit successfully. Well here's some good news: there are a few simple things you can do *right now* to create time in your schedule with hardly any major adjustments. Here's a quick list:

1 Cut your meetings in half.
2 Cut workplace stressors.
3 Cut the clutter.
4 Cut bad habits (and swap in the good).

Do these seem like the sorts of things that are easy enough to say but very difficult to do in the real world? They won't be as hard as you think. Let's take a closer at each one.

1. Cut your meetings in half

There's a saying in education that goes "great teachers don't cover material, they uncover it." You may be the most knowledgeable person in the room, but if the members of your team can't translate your knowledge into action, it means nothing. As a leader, you have the ability to transfer your knowledge to your team by adequately training them. This is your responsibility. Having effective training meetings that uncover understanding, inspire individuals, and build unity will allow your employees to do what needs to be done.

That said, any issue that can be addressed in writing should be—cancel that meeting and send an email or post it to the appropriate Slack channel. Don't meet just to meet. If you're doing your job right, your people have better things to do with their time. The COVID-19 pandemic truly highlighted this: the encroaching "Zoom fatigue" that set in as the months of video meetings dragged on was true motivation to communicate things as quickly and simply as possible—more often than not, through a good old-fashioned email.

Have you ever watched a millennial or a Gen Z employee scroll through their Instagram or Facebook feed, taking in posts and pictures and content faster than the speed of light?

The younger generations have grown up in a world where they can get the information they need very quickly and move on to the next thing. Your message will be better received and will be conveyed more efficiently in a more condensed form than if you stretch it out into an hour-long meeting.

Obviously, sometimes you do need a meeting. But don't think you can't simplify it, no matter what the topic. Cut it in half. Yes, trying to cover too much information in too short a time will result in inefficient retention, but change what's covered, not the meeting length. Take a hard look at what absolutely needs to be there, make a strict (short!) agenda, and throw out the rest. Start and end on time. Ask your team for ideas on how to make it more effective. Communicate clear actions that are understood. Discuss. Laugh. Then release people to do what they do best. Trust me, they'll notice.

2. Cut workplace stressors

For many, a job is just a means to an end. They endure grueling weeks of work merely to get to their annual vacation. Think about the last few times you scrolled Facebook or Instagram. How many memes or posts have you seen about hating Mondays, or "TGIF"?

The American Institute of Stress reports that 80 percent of workers feel stress on the job, and nearly half need help managing stress.[2] They also say that 76 percent of adults cite work/money as the source of their stress.[3] Excessive stress interferes with your employees' productivity and performance. More importantly, it can affect their physical and emotional health, which in turn affects their relationships with colleagues.

In my undercover research, I've seen five factors that are often the largest source of stress for employees:

- . A rigid and controlling manager
- Low salary
- Excessive workload
- Lack of support or friendship from colleagues
- Limited prospects for growth or advancement

Not only is a great manager aware of when situations like these are developing, they also take the initiative to help reduce them.

Will you be able to alleviate all stress for your employees? No, of course not. There are factors that will always be out of your control. But you can still do your part. Even small things can make a big difference. For example, try giving your employees the freedom to set up, organize, decorate, or even paint their own workspaces. The more personalized their space, the more comfortable they will feel. (And don't forget to include your company values and purpose as part of the decor.)

Remember the employee at Weave whose mind was on the need to care for his son and support his family in a challenging time? Even if the need is not dire, flexible work schedules can take a lot of pressure off your employees— most of us have times when events outside of our work life are putting a lot of pressure on our days. If you can't offer a fully flexible schedule, try offering an "early out" day. Take one day a week, maybe Friday, and let your employees go home early—say, 3:30 instead of 5 p.m.

And if all else fails, hold a puppy play day. I'm actually kind of serious: this can be a fail-proof trick (allergies excepted) for releasing pent-up stress in the workplace. The journal *Hypertension* has even reported that dogs reduce their human companions' blood pressure during times of mental stress.[4] Harness that adorable super-powered cuteness by holding

By small and simple things, **great things always come to pass**.

weekly or monthly bring-your-pet-to-work days. In some cities, you can even work with a local rescue or therapy animal group to "rent" some fluffy stress-relievers for a few hours.

3. Cut the clutter

An unorganized or unkempt office environment affects employees' esteem, along with their value for the company. If shared spaces (bathrooms, breakrooms, stairways, supply areas, copy rooms) are not kept clean, you are conveying the message that your employees are not worth investing in. Unclean environments have been connected with higher stress levels, and, as Princeton researchers discovered, clutter can reduce a person's ability to focus on a particular task.[5] Nobody should trip on a stack of copy paper near the doorway.

KonMari that place if you need to. (I highly recommend googling Marie Kondo if you are unfamiliar with her method.)

Now that you've uncluttered your workplace, you are in a better position to work with your employees to create an overall office environment that feels comfortable. Open some windows. Bring in some bright colors, and remove clutter and unnecessary objects where you can in order to create empty spaces that give the eye a rest. Improve the lighting. According to the *Journal of Clinical Sleep Medicine*, employees working in offices with natural light slept an average of 46 minutes longer at night than those working in offices with artificial light or in windowless environments.[6] That translates to more productivity and less stress.

4. Cut bad habits (and swap in the good)

Exercise is an age-old stress buster. A study published in the *Scandinavian Journal of Medicine & Science in Sports* found that people who walked during their lunch breaks at least three times a week were less tense, more enthusiastic, and more relaxed at work.[7] They also found they could cope better with their workloads on the days they walked. Consider organizing lunchtime or afternoon walking groups in your office to reset those mid-day doldrums.

It might also be time to question some of those office standards that are so much a part of our environment that we don't think about them. The scent of coffee brewing in the morning is an established part of the office atmosphere, but too much caffeine consumption can actually increase a person's anxiety, thus reducing their effectiveness. A study from the Duke University Department of Psychiatry showed that those who habitually consumed caffeine (coffee, or even energy drinks) doubled their levels of the stress hormones cortisol and epinephrine.[8] So why do we think of coffee as such a given?

I'm not saying you should forbid coffee in your workplace (prepare for revolution), but consider offering other ways to perk people up. Make sure everyone has easy access to plenty of water to drink. Hangry employees are stressed employees, so keep healthy snacks nearby, and make sure your kitchen or even your vending machines are full of good choices that won't lead to a blood sugar crash.

You could even consider bringing in the occasional yoga or meditation instructor from the local community. Massage schools are always looking for a place for their students to practice—why not bring them in for a few hours now and then to give your employees a well-deserved treat?

I KNOW that not all of these suggestions will work for every organization. Perhaps you don't have the financial means to rent puppies or pay a meditation instructor, but you can also try looking inside your own organization. What skills do your employees possess that could contribute to the welfare of your team? Perhaps one of your employees is an avid yogi and would love to teach a class for a slight bump in pay. Don't be afraid to leverage the skills of your people to better their experience, and everyone's environment.

When I was growing up, my mother always said, "Clint, little by little makes a little a lot, and by small and simple things, great things always come to pass." Keep it simple. Quit the stuff that doesn't work; stick to the stuff that does. Simplify your schedule, your agendas, and your work environment, and invest that earned time into your relationship with your employees. Little by little, those small, casual conversations or thoughtful words of encouragement will become the big things: loyalty, devotion, and respect. You may not remember all the little things you do, but your people will, and they will never forget you for it.

MASTERING YOUR MOMENTS

Question #1: How can you simplify your company vision/mission statement so that it becomes more memorable?

Question #2: How can you simplify your agendas and reduce stress for yourself and for your employees? What can you put on your "to don't" list?

Question #3: How can you make yourself more accessible to your employees and better share your time with them?

Challenge: Say goodbye to stress
Identify five ways you can reduce stress for yourself and your employees, and implement two of those actions right away. Ask your employees what creates the most stress for them in the workplace. Listen to their suggestions and work together on creating a stress-free environment.

Suddenly, things that
didn't seem to
matter to me before
mattered a great deal.

— 7 —

GIVE THEM THE WHEEL AND LET THEM DRIVE

**Having learned it is not as good as having
seen it carried out; having seen it is not
as good as understanding it; understanding
it is not as good as doing it.**

XUNZI

WHEN I WAS ten years old, my dad let me drive home from church for the first time. We lived in a small town, surrounded by a lot of land, so things like this weren't out of the ordinary. My dad put me on his lap and gave me control of the steering wheel while he controlled the gas pedal and the brakes. I was not skilled at steering—the car veered from one side of the road to the other, and my father had to steady it at times—but I didn't mind. The feeling of movement as the car drifted forward filled my small frame with excitement. It was another one of those moments when I was totally present—totally living.

Call it adventurous, call it bad parenting, call it a bonding moment, call it what you will, but I'll never forget what it felt like to take control and "drive" the car for the first time. (Even if I was only steering, it felt like really driving to me.) I had been in that car hundreds of times with my parents, riding to and from all sorts of places. I knew the feeling of the car's motion, the acceleration, the pull of winding curves, the jolt of a sudden stop. But this time was different: my young mind registered an importance, a new responsibility, a next level of living. I had a greater appreciation, I was more attentive and aware, and, suddenly, things that didn't seem to matter to me before mattered a great deal—the sidewalks, the winding and steep roads, the creek that ran along the side of the street. Even stop signs, yield signs, and street names that I had never really noticed before came into sharp focus.

Ownership is a game changer. I discovered this when I was steering that car at the age of ten, and many happy employees I have interviewed discovered it when their leaders provided them with the opportunity to take control over their part in steering the company where it needs to go. Giving your employees this kind of ownership builds trust, provides a greater sense of purpose and meaning, and opens the door for better mentorship. Much like driver's ed, it's a perfect training course to help you guide your employees to success.

When employees take ownership of their work, it completely changes the way they treat the business they work for—and the way they treat its money. There's a shift in perspective that takes them from "I work here" to "I'm building something here."

A story I think about often illustrates this perfectly. It took place 1961, when President John F. Kennedy announced his vision to send Americans to the moon and bring them back again, and to do it within the decade. The Soviets had already started the "space race" with the launch of cosmonaut Yuri Gagarin the previous month, and President Kennedy felt that the U.S. was greatly behind. America waited with great anticipation for NASA to announce their newest launches as the excitement of exploring the moon swept the nation. The first time President Kennedy visited NASA, he said he was impressed by the dedication of the engineers and technicians and the courage of the astronauts, but one person impressed him the most: a humble janitor.

While the janitor was mopping the floor in one of the hallways, the president decided to introduce himself. The janitor gleefully shook the president's hand, honored at the opportunity to be in his presence. "What do you do here?" asked President Kennedy. The janitor smiled. "Well," he said, "I'm helping put a man on the moon."

When a person takes ownership, things matter more. They become more driven and motivated, take more initiative, and seek creative and innovative ways to improve what they're doing. When an employee is invested in their work in this way, they no longer coast or go through the motions; they become more intentional about their time and experience, and they're more present each day. The working environment becomes positive, productive, and uplifting—even for managers. In short, a company with employees who are given the opportunity to take ownership is a company that is moving forward.

Once again, I'm going to try to read your mind. Likely, what I've said so far has triggered a few questions:

- Sounds good, but *how* do I give my employees ownership?
- Am I supposed to give them stock or equity in the company?
- Is ownership the same thing as responsibility?
- What if I don't trust my employees with more responsibility?

Let me take the last question first: if you don't trust your employees with more responsibility, then perhaps you've hired the wrong people. Or maybe you don't yet know your employees well enough to assess their character and capabilities. If that's the case, start there: get to know your people, and make sure *they* can trust *you*. And keep in mind that cultivating ownership is not all-or-nothing, nor is it tossing your people into the deep end of the pool and seeing whether they sink or swim. Start small, experiment and evaluate, change your approach as needed, and build on successes.

Now, let's take a step back to the other three questions.

Making an Environment of Ownership

For some employees, a sense of ownership might come naturally. With those who have a take-charge mindset, you can focus more on providing guidance and direction. For others, that sense of ownership must be fostered. Even without things like profit-sharing or equity (we'll address that soon), there are plenty of ways to cultivate a sense of ownership, both in individual employees and in your work culture as a whole. A lot of the great initiatives I've seen can be organized into five categories:

1 Enable your employees to act.
2 Involve your team in hiring decisions.
3 Allow flexible schedules.
4 Ask for ideas.
5 Delegate responsibility.

Let me give you some real-world examples to show you the incredible effect each of these small investments in trust and empowerment can make.

A company with **employees who are given the opportunity to take ownership** is a company that is moving forward.

1. Enable your employees to act

Organizations can create a culture of ownership by giving employees the autonomy to help clients in whatever ways seem appropriate. One of the better examples I have seen of this was done by Rob Ferrell, a successful dental surgeon and a fantastic leader. Rob has always strived to be in tune with the concerns and needs of his organization and the people involved. He's created a culture in his office in which all of his employees have the freedom to provide imaginative and caring customer service, in the hopes of creating a greater experience for his customers. One of the ways he facilitated this was by setting up a cash box in which he keeps money, gift cards, candy, and other miscellaneous items. This box and its contents are available to everyone on his staff to use for whatever purpose they feel is necessary to serve their customers and make them feel taken care of.

Rob did this for a couple of reasons. First, most of his day is spent with his hands in people's mouths. He doesn't have time to greet patients at the door, talk on the phone through somebody's dental emergency, or maintain face-to-face contact while handling scheduling, follow-ups, and so on. Rob knows his strengths and focuses on the work that he does best. He relies on his entire staff to treat clients the way *he* would want them treated, and he gives them the freedom and autonomy to do so without repercussions.

On one occasion, a woman came into the dental clinic who had been suffering for years with periodontal infections and was slowly losing her teeth. She had expressed several times the ongoing blow this was having to her self-esteem, and how it made it hard to smile (or even wish to smile). It had also caused some complications that had restricted her from eating any type of solid food for over twenty years. "I would give anything to be able to eat corn on the cob again!" she said at one of her initial appointments.

After several visits, which included getting implants, the woman started showing up to her appointments with a smile on her face—one that grew bigger and bigger each time as she proudly showed off her teeth and her healing gums. On the way out of her last dental appointment, one of Rob's employees stopped her at the door and graciously handed her a bag. Inside the bag were twelve fresh ears of corn.

The woman began to weep at the gesture. Not only was her mouth almost fully healed, she also couldn't believe that her dental surgeon's assistants had *listened*, and had *remembered* something that seemed like such a small passing comment. Yes, it had been small, but it had so much value to her, and this assistant had noticed that. She hugged the young employee and each of the staff members, and went back to hug Rob before she left the office for the final time. "I'll tell everyone about you!" she cried as she left.

And she has.

It's important to note that this young employee did not perform this gesture for a better review from a satisfied customer or to get the word out about their dental office. She did it because her employer had enabled her to take ownership and make decisions about what it took to care deeply for their patients. When the woman came back to hug Rob, he was unaware that his employee had taken money from the cash box and slipped out for fifteen minutes to buy some corn for his patient. He also was unaware that his staff had heard the patient speak of her love for corn. But he didn't need to—his employees knew they were empowered to serve and care for their clients in whatever ways they felt would make a difference.

2. Involve your team in hiring decisions

Rather than leave hiring exclusively to the hiring managers, innovative companies often bring their wider staff into that process. We've noticed that simply having an employee sit in on the interview process and weigh in on the decision-making produces a great amount of ownership. One major tech company we've worked with in our undercover research has this as part of their standard interview process, and it was often raised by employees as something they appreciated. A job candidate's first interview is with two members of the team they would be working with. Those frontline employees are the ones who decide:

- Whether they feel confident in having this candidate on their team

- Whether the candidate deserves a second interview (which then involves upper management)

If your organization doesn't typically conduct multiple interviews with each candidate, you can still find ways to include employees in the hiring process. Give them opportunities to listen and be present during interviews. Encourage them to ask the candidates questions, and make sure you listen to your employees' feedback after the interviews. Are those employees now totally responsible for hiring the right individual? Of course not. But do they have some influence and a sense of ownership in the process? You bet.

3. Allow flexible schedules

I touched on this in the previous chapter, but it's worth mentioning again here. The days of working a strict 9-to-5 schedule, five days a week, are quickly fading away. With the disruption of COVID-19, many teams were forced into remote environments, and "normal" work schedules disappeared completely—an event that highlighted both how much workplaces need to be prepared for the unexpected, and how much (it turns out) we can flex when we need to.

Employees are now looking for and needing more flexibility to meet the various demands both inside and outside the workplace. Our research has shown that significant leaders who value and understand that employees have a life outside of their work are consistently cherished and appreciated by their workforce. Instead of enforcing a strict schedule according to past ideals and expectations, let your people dictate their own schedules. Give them ownership of their time. Certainly there are deadlines to be met and parameters that need to be maintained—meetings to be attended, appointments to be kept, communication that needs to happen. But if employees can meet (and perhaps exceed) your expectations for performance and collaboration while varying their schedules, that flexibility can go a long way in retaining their loyalty.

A leader we worked with told us that one of her employees has been granted the ability to never be at the office past 4:30 p.m. Why? He wants to go fishing. He wants to walk his dogs. These things are really important to him. "He gets his work done quickly, and he's fine with making a little less money if he doesn't hit forty hours a week," she told us. To provide that flexibility, she said, "you really do have to know your employees; there has to be really good, safe communication." The arrangement works: that employee has been with the organization for seventeen years.

4. Ask for ideas

As you brainstorm ways to let your employees drive the car, consider asking them what *they* think they could take charge of, and what that might look like. As I've said before, simply asking an employee how they'd like to contribute is a perfect way to begin a trusting relationship. From there, you can start collaborating on ideas that will ultimately give them more ownership over what they do. Our interviews have shown us again and again that employees want dialogue. They want to be listened to. If you have an open mind and work together with your staff, you'll likely find a few areas in which you can feel confident giving them ownership.

5. Delegate responsibility

Sometimes you don't even need to ask; you just need to listen when your employees come to you and ask to take charge of something. (Of course, it's still your job to decide whether they have the necessary skills—and to provide them with opportunities for training or guidance if they don't.) Remember Jeanette from Bennett Communications? Her employee "Chelsea" had been working with the company for a few years and expressed interest in becoming an editor. Says Jeanette: "She wanted to really wrap her arms around an industry or a project... she just had this dream of being the face of something." Jeanette ended up working one-one-one with Chelsea to produce an issue of the annual *Utah Valley Bride* magazine so that Chelsea could earn the skills and experience to take it over the next year.

Chelsea also had a goal for the magazine's Instagram account: she wanted to be in charge of it, be the voice for it, and post more often than the company had been posting. And she wanted to hit 100,000 followers. Given the magazine's budget, Jeanette told her she probably couldn't compensate her for the level of effort it would take. Chelsea said she wanted to put the effort in anyway. As of this writing, the account has almost 99,000 followers, and Jeanette makes sure that the company celebrates any milestones they hit.

The Link Between Ownership and Responsibility

Here I should note that, even though responsibility and ownership do go together, they aren't the same thing. Just as I was a ten-year-old boy who was too young, could barely see over the steering wheel, couldn't touch the pedals, and had no driving experience, you'll find that not all of your employees are equipped to immediately handle bigger responsibilities on their own. When my dad gave me the wheel, I had some of the responsibility, but I didn't have all of it—my "driving" had limits, and the rest was handled by my father—but holding the steering wheel, even under supervision, allowed me to see things from a new perspective. I knew that I had made a pretty substantial impact on the outcome of our day.

When a leader delegates to her team, she doesn't abdicate all responsibility. There is still oversight, guidance, and accountability that needs to take place. It's possible to give your people both, while not feeling like you're losing control.

One manager we spoke with—"Kris," who worked for twelve years in hospital administration—told us that when she's ready to delegate some responsibility, she's careful to do a few things:

> I make sure that they know my expectation: this is what needs to happen, this is the end goal. I always let them know that I believe in them and their abilities, and that's why I asked them. And then I say, "You own it, you do it. You do it your way."

She always makes sure to mention specific experiences that have shown that the employee has what it takes to take on the new responsibility. And Kris has seen the benefits of this kind of delegation:

I think that burnout is at a minimum because they're really believing, and doing something that they feel good about. Because it's theirs.

That sense of ownership will also determine how your employees talk about their jobs to others. Do you want employees who feel like they are just laying bricks, or employees who are excited to tell their friends about how they are building a company?

Often, it can be difficult to hand over ownership, especially when it comes to the projects that are most important to you. However, those big items can create the motivation that will allow your employees to expand their vision of what's possible and reach a new potential. That doesn't mean just passing along the grunt work or tasks you don't want to do. The work you hand over needs to be something they can take pride in, something of significance. Ownership should be an opportunity, *not* a curse. Make it worth their while. Remember, the point is to help them grow while furthering the company's goals. If the task doesn't make them stretch, then consider offering something more.

So many people feel bogged down in the world of work. Others feel harried, like the dogs are barking and the sirens are blaring. When we're faced with the chaos of life, it's hard not to drop to our knees and say, "I can't do any more." You have the power to show your tired employees a bigger picture that will shake them out of their boredom; you can give your distracted employees the understanding that stress can be a moment they pass through on the way to something more important. By letting your employees drive the car, you invest them in getting to where the company is going—even if it's as far as the moon and back.

MASTERING YOUR MOMENTS

Question #1: How is your organization creating an ownership environment?

Question #2: How can you encourage your employees to take ownership in their work?

Question #3: What are some things that you can let go of and let your employees take on instead?

Challenge: Build the bigger picture
Determine what the bigger picture is for your organization and list the individual building blocks that make up that picture. Identify what part is yours, and what you can give to others. Make a list of your employees or immediate team members and determine what building block each one could carry to provide them with a sense of ownership. Make adjustments if necessary.

It was hard to understand how planes of the same make and model could be different—**until we were actually flying them**.

— 8 —

ALWAYS BE FLYING THE AIRPLANE

Leadership is an action, not a position.

DONALD MCGANNON

JUST WHEN I have you thinking "wheels on the road," let me take you back up into the air for a moment. When I was in flight school, one of the first lessons they taught me was that no two planes fly exactly the same. For this reason, we trained in multiples of the same aircraft—same make, same model, same height, same weight, same engine. It was hard to understand how planes of the same make and model could be different—until we were actually flying them. They all had their own feel, their own energy, their own strengths and weaknesses. Some would accelerate faster than others, some would stall out at different speeds, and some would shift or steer more smoothly.

Every plane came with the same manual, providing the same specifications, but every pilot knew that the manual could never replace actually getting in and flying the plane.

Understanding each plane required time, patience, feeling, intuition, and practice.

Learning the mechanics of flying a plane is just the starting point. During every flight, you must stay alert, evaluate changing conditions, and immediately correct when necessary to maintain a clear and safe course. The medical field requires a similar kind of situational awareness, in which you're frequently evaluating a patient's status. If you've ever watched a medical drama on television, you've seen an ambulance crew calling out a patient's vital signs—body temperature, blood pressure, heart rate, respiratory rate. The medics have to know exactly what's happening with the patient in order to properly treat them. It's the same scenario at the hospital: doctors check and recheck each patient's status, helping them determine the best course of action.

Check signs—evaluate—determine action—take action—check signs—evaluate—determine action—take action. This pattern continues until the patient is stable or the plane is on the ground.

It's similar with mentorship in the workplace. One of your goals as a leader should always be achieving and maintaining healthy stability for your employees. You should constantly be asking yourself: "Are they stable—are they in a place where they can continue to grow and thrive in their work environment?" Because, as a leader, not only do you get to help create that work environment, you are also responsible for sustaining it. You want to keep your employees *here*, both physically and mentally—to keep them from quitting emotionally or from actually walking out the door. So, like the doctor, like the pilot, observe and adjust: check status—evaluate—determine needs—create action plan—check status—evaluate—determine needs—create action plan... and so on. Constantly, for each employee.

One of the best things that great Mentor Managers consistently do to create this observation cycle is to regularly conduct what I like to call "the status interview." (This is especially true for employees who you really want to keep.) The purpose of a status interview is to check the vitals of an employee *before it's too late*. This is not a performance review or a traditional one-on-one meeting. It's not about the company's goals; it's about the employee's. The focus of a status interview is on advocating for the employee—asking them what they need or what you can do for them. After you determine their needs through thoughtful questioning (which we will get into in a moment), you can create an action plan to help address those needs.

The status interview is one more way for you to connect with your employees and keep them feeling valued and engaged. Don't make the mistake of thinking these interviews are just for frontline or entry-level employees. These should be conducted with every member of your organization, from management all the way up to the executive team.

You have to know what your employees' needs are so that you can create a plan that will help them grow into who and what they want to become—if you neglect this, your employees will leave and grow somewhere else. Like airplanes, no two status interviews will be the same, and no two employees will have the same needs—you have to get to know them individually. You won't be able to get an accurate gauge of how they work, what their needs are, or how you can help them unless you are constantly "flying the airplane."

Think of status interviews as a way to create the map—a solid understanding of the landscape, the peaks and valleys, the boggy bits, the riverways that will make progress fast and easy. Once you have that picture, you can plan your route. That's your growth development plan.

We'll get into growth development plans in much more detail later in this chapter—they've helped many of the companies we've worked with increase loyalty and retention, foster deeper engagement, and improve the connection between co-workers. But first, we need to talk a little bit more about status interviews, and making that map. Status interviews don't necessarily need to be planned out, but they do need to be authentic, and repeated. The better you understand the status of your people, the longer they will stay and engage with your organization.

How to Hold a Successful Status Interview

If you want your status interview to have value, it's crucial to first establish an element of trust between you and your team (which, as you know from chapter four, happens as you work to become a connected Mentor Manager, with high expectations and high connection). This is why it's essential to understand that the status interview is not the time to place blame or discuss performance issues. It's simply a way to check the status of your people, and create action plans.

Your status interview does not have to be a long meeting, nor should you bombard the employee with a lot of questions. This is a friendly conversation, not an interrogation—but, that said, it's also a formal and planned moment. Keep it simple. In our experience, there is a narrow set of questions that have the best results in terms of getting useful insight into an individual employee:

1 What can we do to keep you here?
2 What's getting in the way of reaching your maximum success level?
3 How can I help you get where you want to go?

Of course, there's a bit more to it than just ticking off these questions and sending them on their way. Let's look a little closer at what you're trying to achieve with each of these questions.

1. What can we do to keep you here?

Before you even ask this question, you must first begin with some vocal praise, and acknowledge that the reason you're having this meeting is because of the value that they bring to the organization. When was the last time you sat down with your valued employee and said, "Hey, you are really important to this company, and I want to make sure that you've got what you need to be successful. What can we do to keep you here?" Beginning with some sort of praise alleviates any nervousness or tension, and immediately clarifies to the employee that your intention is to keep them, not to stress them out or make them worried that you suspect them of looking elsewhere.

It's funny, because questions like this are usually posed only during exit interviews, when an employee has already decided to leave. What a poorly chosen time to learn the answer! Asking this while your employee is still engaged in their work will show them they are valued, and keep them loyal to you and your company.

2. What's getting in the way of reaching your maximum success level?

When was the last time you asked an employee what obstacles they were facing as they pursued their goals? Are there skills they want to learn? Does their schedule work well for them, or does it need some adjusting? Do they need help with a personal or family issue? If so, can you provide referrals to the appropriate professionals? An effective leader is always looking to help improve their employees' skills and help them succeed, both in and out of the office.

But before you ask this question of your employee, check in with yourself first! Are you prepared to hear an answer that may seem critical of your workplace, or even of your leadership? How will you react if you do? An interview with the boss—even a friendly one—can be a stressful experience for an employee, and they likely don't want to wound your feelings or turn you against them. If you want to fortify a sense of trust, it is absolutely critical that you do not react defensively to feedback you receive—an angry or hurt response to anything they tell you (or, worse, any form of retribution down the line) will be the kiss of death for their ability to feel confident in being honest and open with you.

3. How can I help you get where you want to go?

When you're a mentor, your job is to connect your people to their dreams, whether within the company or outside of it. This question is important because it puts you in the position of the advocate. When an employee feels fulfilled in life, they're less likely to seek out life changes that will take them away from your company. True, a person's fulfillment may ultimately be found elsewhere. But even in such a case, many people can find fulfillment in side pursuits that could be balanced with their work. If it still turns out that the company really isn't compatible with their life goals, it's better to find that out sooner rather than later. More often, though, the employee is working at your business because something attracted them to that type of work. Tapping back into that energy will help increase their drive to succeed.

And remember: another beauty of knowing where your employee wants to go is that you can play to those strengths, and find opportunities within the company to help them feel fulfilled and moving in the direction of their dreams.

When you're a mentor, your job is to **connect your people to their dreams.**

THE STATUS interview may be all about the employee, but that doesn't mean you're not a big part of this meeting. There are a few simple ways to help your employees see that you're listening to them, and you're willing to understand and validate what they're saying.

One clearly visible way to do this is to take notes. It's important for your employees to see you physically recording what they are saying. I encourage you to do this on paper. Of course, it's not just for show: making handwritten notes helps you capture their ideas and comments, gives you an easy way to refer back to them (in our experience, physical, paper notes are both easier and more likely to be referred to later than digital ones), and—perhaps most importantly—involves a sense of care and intentionality that will help you better pay attention and process what you are hearing.

If the pen-and-paper method doesn't work for you, then by all means type away. But writing notes on paper is a simple yet valuable practice that happy employees have reported to us as something they appreciate. But however you make your notes, don't forget to pull them out and refresh your memory before any later interviews with that employee.

There's one more tip I'd like to pass on to help make your status interviews more effective: repeat what the employee is saying. I don't mean you should come off like a robot, but you should listen closely to your employee, and repeat their concerns and needs. That way, both you and your employee will know for certain exactly what those needs and concerns are, and you will both understand them in the same way.

If there is a misunderstanding, restate your understanding of their concern. This will identify any confusion and provide an opportunity for clarification. If they know that you understand them, they will know you care. This simple practice, called "active listening," is a key to effective communication. With it, you will both have a clear vision of your common goal.

"The Script"—aka the Growth Development Plan

After you do a status interview, it's crucial to write out the plan. Let me go back to a medical analogy again: when a doctor has diagnosed a patient, often they won't just scribble off an Rx, or drug prescription. When a bigger health goal is at stake, they will create a bigger kind of "script": a treatment plan, laying out the simple, measurable, and outcome-oriented steps the doctor and patient will take together to get the result they both want.

A growth development plan is like you writing this kind of script for your employee. It should be inspiring, realistic, and always associated with time. And it should always include the following:

- A clear statement of the goal you set together

- The actions you will take as a manager to reach that goal

- The actions the employee will take themselves to reach that goal

- The dates by which these actions will be completed, and when a follow-up meeting will take place

Copies of this growth development plan should be made for both you and your employee. This script will make it clear that you're working with the employee as a partnership. It will also communicate to the employee that you value their success.

Okay, once again, I know what some of you are thinking: "But what if I can't give them what they want?" What if they ask for a corner office, or ski passes, more Cheetos, those

What if they ask for a corner office, or ski passes, or more Cheetos?

weird hot Cheetos, fancy bean bags, or a higher salary and end-of-year bonus? Or, worse, what if they haven't proven merit equal to what they're asking for?

Let's take the money requests first: your response to these can be much simpler than you think. Here are a few great examples:

- How much more do you think you should be making? What kind of numbers did you have in mind?

- What actions could you take (or have you taken) to justify an increase in pay?

- What skills can you develop to help you add more value to the company? And how can we help you develop those skills?

It's important to remember that when an employee asks for an increase in pay, it's not always founded in wanting more wealth. Oftentimes, what the employee is really asking for is acknowledgment of their worth and potential, in accordance with what feels true to them, so recognizing and supporting that potential can do the trick. Of course, you can make your decisions accordingly.

And whether it's money or a bean bag or a trip or super-hot Cheetos on tap, if you can't provide what they're asking for, you can still communicate their value to the organization. Be honest. It's perfectly acceptable to say something like, "We just can't do that right now" or "This is the limitation that prevents us from being able to do that." Then, ask for an alternative: "Is there something else we can do?" Sometimes they'll have an answer—maybe a few more vacation days, more flex time, or the ability to work from home one day a week. Sometimes they won't. Either way, you have asked, they have spoken, and you have listened. That's the beauty of a status interview. It allows your employees to recognize that they've been heard.

I've done a fair amount of undercover research in the automotive industry, and one of the great opportunities I've had was to work with a large retail tire chain, interviewing a couple hundred of their employees nationwide (you may remember that I've referred to this chain before). In all of my research and interviews, it's been the leaders I've met who model the Mentor Manager style and create true significance in the workplace who truly stand out as special people; they have good hearts, and always a genuine love for others. One of these leaders was an owner of one of that tire chain's franchises.

"Frank" looked rough on the outside, but was one of the most genuine and authentic leaders I have ever had the pleasure of meeting. Everyone loved him. He had almost taken on the role of a father figure for the individuals who worked for him. He was more than a boss to his employees, and to him, they were his kids.

Going undercover into this tire store was like walking into a family reunion. There was a feeling of community, love, and siblinghood. It was fun, vibrant, and full of like-minded individuals on a mission to keep people safe and have fun while doing it. Frank's tire store was famous among his customers for writing handwritten thank-you cards and putting them on the customer's dashboard when they were done with their tire service. These cards would always personally thank the customer for their trust in the store and for their loyalty as a customer.

Frank's retention rates were some of the highest we had ever seen in the auto industry, averaging ten years of employment for most of the employees in his store. When I asked Frank the secret behind this consistent loyalty from his people, he simply said, "I just try to listen, and I try to remember, and I try to make sure that they know that I remember." This was profound to me: it's one thing to "listen" as a leader, but it's another to communicate that you remember—and value—what was said.

Frank showed me the inside of his office, where there was a corkboard with eight pictures attached to it. I asked him about them, and he said, "These are the dreams of my team. What matters to them matters to me."

He pointed to a picture in the top-left corner of the board—it was of a couple holding a baby, whom he said represented "Ben" and "Heather." He went on: "This year, Ben and Heather are trying to raise money to help with infertility issues, so we're working with Ben on different ways that we can put a little extra money into his paycheck every month to help make that happen," he told me. On the bottom-left corner of the board was a picture of a fishing boat. "Steve," he said, loved to fish. "So we're working together to make sure we can help him get a better fishing boat."

He then talked about "Riley" and "Melissa," who were represented in the middle of the board by a picture of a home. They were working toward saving up for a down payment on their first house. Next to that was a picture of the sandy beaches of Hawaii, which was important to "Carl," the head technician. "I'm hoping to help take his family on a much-needed vacation," said Frank.

Finally, I noticed a picture of another tire store. That picture was for "Ray," who dreamed of managing his own store one day, just like Frank. How cool is that?

I asked Frank how he found out all of this information, and he said, "I just talk with them regularly. I make sure to chat with each of them privately about how they're doing, what they're doing, what they're needing, and what they're hoping for. It could be about anything. Sometimes it's about work, sometimes it's about life. It doesn't matter what we talk about, because if it's important to them, it's important to me."

Frank's goal was not just to provide great customer service and run a great tire store, but also to help his people get what they wanted in life. It mattered to his employees that Frank kept a "dream board" for them, and, more importantly, the contents of that dream board mattered to Frank.

Frank told me that any time he chatted with an employee (or held a status interview if they were discussing work) and they expressed a dream, he would create a simple four-by-six picture of that dream, and hang it up so they could both see "the main thing" that they could work toward together. He also encouraged them to keep a similar picture in their own workstation to help them remember their goal too.

This small action kept that employee's vision alive—kept *the main thing the main thing*. Frank loved when one of his employees would hit their goal, reach their dream, or achieve whatever milestone it was that they were wanting, and he made sure that every milestone was celebrated and acknowledged by the team. This allowed everyone to know what mattered to everyone else, increasing both the overall morale of the team and the culture of unity Frank was striving to create.

There Are No Shortcuts

Something fascinating I have observed and studied while working undercover is to see how much surveys and other personality assessments were used as mandatory onboarding, corporate training, and even team building exercises for current and potential employees and management. One of these popular assessments is called the Hartman Color Code. Many of you will be familiar with this test, but here's a refresher

There are no shortcuts to learning about your people.

for those who aren't: individuals are categorized into specific colors based on how they answer a series of questions, which are meant to trigger inward discovery through subjective observation. Through this process, you can supposedly open a window into what you weren't able to see before.

The unique part of this particular test is that, while answering the questions, you're required to respond as if you were your child-like self: "When I was a child, if somebody asked me this question, what would my response have been?" You give your answer, the results dictate which color(s) you are, and that gives you a guide to who you are as a person, and how you're likely to handle certain situations. In essence, this test is designed to give people a deeper understanding of why they do the things they do, and how they might best treat others and approach the events in their life.

Now, I fully support the idea of looking inward and learning more about yourself as a resource for personal betterment, but I have seen this test create an interesting dynamic within the various groups. When introductions are made, the first thing asked is often, "What color are you?" Communication and conversation then proceeds, but the tone is dependent on their answers. I have watched as suddenly management and co-workers came to feel like they had an immediate and thorough understanding of each person. At times, participants will question what they know about themselves based on the color assigned to them. On the surface, this Color Code test (and personality assessments in general) seem fairly harmless, but they tend to put us in a box and keep us there.

If the results of these tests are properly understood and used as a guide, I believe they can be helpful, to a degree. But I don't believe it to be an accurate and all-knowing diagnosis; nor do I believe that a "code" or any similar system can replace the power of authentic connection and communication. Just like a survey cannot replace an honest conversation, a personality test cannot determine how people need to be treated. There are no shortcuts to learning about your people. This is why a status interview needs to happen with each team member, and on an individual basis. To go back to that "no two airplanes" analogy, no two employees will ever be the same.

If you can learn and apply the core principles in this chapter and take the time to truly understand your employees, you'll be well on your way to a more successful organization. Remember, you are the pilot, the captain, the one who is charting a course on the map for every person on your team. So never put your employees in a box—ask them directly who they are and what they want. Take the time to really listen, and show that what they say is important to you. Handle your employees with care, because you can't succeed without them, and they can't succeed without you.

MASTERING YOUR MOMENTS

Question #1: How can you successfully implement status interviews within your organization?

Question #2: Think back to Frank the tire store owner. What can you do to make sure your employees know that you remember what matters to them?

Question #3: Have you put your employees in a box in terms of your view of them? How?

Challenge: Create healthy stability

Review the list of questions you can ask in a status interview (page 140) to determine the needs and desires of your employees. Then, schedule a status interview with each one to determine how they're doing and what they need in order reach their maximum potential. Create a growth development plan with each employee, and a timeline for a follow-up review. And remember: always keep your hackles down, and your ears open.

If there's one thing the past few years have given us, **it's plenty of crisis to learn from**.

— 9 —

BRACE FOR IMPACT

A crisis is a terrible thing to waste.

PAUL ROMER

L ET'S SAY that you've worked your way through the previous chapters and taken the challenges to heart. You've
hired (or created a plan to hire) some terrific people, or
moved employees into positions they're better suited
for; you've gotten more invested in your people (and vice
versa); you've discussed their goals and dreams; you've got
plans for their professional development; you're all working
toward the organization's vision and your people's individual
needs. Life is good.

Then, suddenly, it's not so good. Maybe there's a short-
term setback; maybe something truly terrible happens—to
an employee or your company or your town. You've hit tur-
bulence. How can you care for your passengers? And what
can you do to either keep the plane aloft or help your people
brace for impact?

Well, if there's one thing the past few years have given us,
it's plenty of crisis to learn from. In my years of undercover
research, I have seen many different approaches to preparing

a company for unexpected events—and, just as importantly, to helping that company's team through those events, or even through an employee's own personal crises. I've also witnessed some very creative and effective solutions that happened on the fly, because, as it turns out, some crises show up without setting an appointment.

In this chapter I'd like to break down some of the best approaches I've seen for preparing a team—and a company—for a crisis, whether the crisis might be on a personal, corporate, or national level. These strategies come from companies that have weathered storms of every scale (and from lessons learned from those that didn't), but not every one of them will apply to you: small businesses don't usually have the financial resources of larger ones, and, as we discovered with COVID-19, not every company can sustain itself through a months-long shutdown.

So, with the guidance I'm about to lay out for you—gathered from many years of observing the mistakes and successes of companies of all sizes—take what will work for your specific situation, and leave the rest. And remember: regardless of how much or little money or resources your organization has, you can always afford to show your employees that you care about them.

When Your Employee Has a Crisis

Picture this: during a conversation with an employee who has been having performance issues, you find out that they're dealing with an abusive partner at home. Or say an employee tells you they've been diagnosed with cancer and will need months of treatment; they'll work when they can, but they'll need multiple days and weeks off at unpredictable intervals.

Or how about this: an employee who's working on a project with a tight deadline tells you there's been a death in the family, and they don't yet know if or when they'll have to travel for a funeral.

No matter how much you care about your people or empathize with their situation, one of your first thoughts will likely be: "How will we get the work done?" or "What about the deadline?" or that old comic-strip standby: "Aaack!" All understandable—and all responses that we've seen play out many times at the start of an unexpected turn of events. But even if this is your first reaction, you'll want to keep it to yourself for the moment. Save it for a later conversation with a trusted advisor.

Employees we've met who love where they work trust that they can go to their manager in a crisis, because they know that person will do what they can to give them what they need—right at the moment of the crisis, as well as later as its effects start playing out. And what they need is this:

Listen. Employees want empathy from their manager, and acknowledgment of the difficulty of their situation. If you have the urge to give advice and jump into fix-it mode (which many of us often do), rein that in.

Remember the power of simple statements and questions. In a moment of personal crisis, great managers ask questions like: "How can we support you right now?" "What do you need?" "How are you feeling today?" "I'm sorry you are going through this."

Maintain confidentiality. If someone comes into your office and says, "Look, I'm having a personal problem," they need to know and trust that your office is a vault. They have to believe that their colleagues won't be privy to that information. If you do need to share information about a situation to get the person more help or find temporary workarounds, *ask their permission first.*

If your employee asks for help, assess what you can realistically do. Many, but not all, of the companies we work with have a formal Employee Assistance Program—if yours has one, that's a good place to start. If your organization doesn't have the resources or expertise needed, maybe you can find out where to get it. Employees we've talked with who have been through a moment like this truly appreciated that extra bit of effort, particularly when they didn't have the time or mental resources to seek out those resources themselves.

Determine what projects and deadlines will be affected, and how. Think about ways to be flexible. Can the employee work from home? If their work requires their presence in the office, can they vary their hours to work around appointments or any other responsibilities related to the crisis? Can someone switch jobs, or particular job duties, with the person who's having a hard time? Who else in the company, or in a network of freelancers, can help out for a while?

Assume that your employee is doing the best they can under difficult circumstances. Nobody wants to be the person who's holding up projects, missing deadlines, or forgetting tasks, so if an assignment is overdue, assume it's an oversight. Evaluate the impact of the delay, and decide whether you need to give the assignment to someone else or just issue a compassionate reminder.

Determine which performance standards (if any) can be relaxed and for how long. The biggest hearts in the world are still bound by the limits of reality. Even the most empathetic Mentor Managers we've seen know that they still have

You can always afford to show your employees that **you care about them**.

a business to run, with customers and other employees relying on them—and, often, on the person who's having issues too. It's okay to check in periodically with the employee, both to see how they're doing and to see if they need help with completing or delegating some assignments.

Determine how long (or whether) you can afford to pay their salaries and health insurance. This is particularly important if there is a chance the employee will need a lot of time off for treatment. When one employee of Böhme (the chain of clothing boutiques I mentioned in chapter five) was diagnosed with cancer and was in and out of the hospital, Fernanda

Böhme was able to continue paying his salary for an entire year. Not every company can do that, of course, but do what you can. If you can't keep paying their salary, can you continue their health insurance for a while? If your business is too small to provide insurance, are there other ways to help? Can you get the person's permission to create a GoFundMe page for them? Can you or co-workers help out with meals or childcare? (Again, it's up to the employee to decide how much information, if any, they want to share with co-workers about their issues or needs.)

Remember—and help them remember—that your employees are more than their illnesses. If an employee is struggling with a serious illness, that illness doesn't have to be the subject of every conversation you have. Do you usually talk about sports or kids or movies with that person? Keep doing that. The best managers see their employees as a whole person. Do that, and they will see themselves that way too.

When Your Company Has a Crisis

What happens when it's not your employee who's having trouble, but the entire company—in the form of a financial setback or crisis? Even the biggest and best companies that we've worked with have hit rough patches and stumbling blocks: losing a big account, facing a reputation issue, or, like all of us, weathering an economic downturn. Some companies have gone through periods where they were doing mostly okay but knew that they would be squeaking by for a while. If you find yourself in that situation, how do you handle the shortfall, and how much do you tell your employees?

Over and over in my research, I've observed the importance of vulnerability, transparency, and honesty in dealing with a

corporate crisis. There's a fine line to be found, certainly—
I've seen some managers share so many details of a temporary
crisis that they unintentionally induced additional anxiety in
their employees—but uncertainty can provoke even more
unease, so chances are good that your employees will appreciate your honesty. They might even be able to help you.

Here's some lived, real-world insight on this from Jeanette
Bennett of Bennett Communications:

> There were some times early on when we were cutting
> it close. A couple of times when we were in that crunch,
> I involved the whole company. I said, "Okay, we need
> $76,000 this week, and people owe us that. So, I need your
> help to call these clients and say, 'Could we get a payment
> today?'" And we made it fun. We divided into teams and
> rang bells and, basically, it turned into a game. And I was
> honest with them. I said, "We're not in trouble, but we
> need to collect this money so that we can pay our bills."

You might worry that if you tell your people the company
is having financial issues, even short-term ones, they'll start
looking for other jobs. That's always possible, but if you've
been working at building trust, your employees will likely
stay put. Jeanette said:

> The first year, I was worried they'd start looking for other
> jobs. But their reaction was so warming and so kind that I
> felt okay about it. So then I was able to do it again, without
> worry. So it was a concern, but I think the opposite actually
> happened. I think they were thinking, "Oh, she's not going
> to close the doors and not give us any warning. She's being
> so honest and open with us, and we want to stay here. And
> it's going to take all of us to solve this temporary problem,
> so let's do it."

Some companies we've worked with have faced serious financial setbacks—and the ones that have the best relationships with their employees were always honest and up front about it, even if the outlook seemed dire. When things get rough, they explain what's going on and how they plan to deal with it, they are honest about the severity of the situation, and they enlist their employees' help whenever they can. If you find yourself in this situation, take the risk of being open with your employees: you might be surprised to see how willing they are to pitch in and what sorts of creative ideas they come up with.

When Your Town—or Country—Has a Crisis

A fire spreads, threatening an area where many of your employees live. A hurricane or tornado flattens part of your town, or a flood puts portions of it underwater. Natural disasters are inevitable. And as if those aren't enough, COVID-19 showed us all how devastating a pandemic can be—physically, emotionally, and economically (and some experts say that new pandemics are a matter of when, not if). Here are some things we've observed that have made a big difference to companies and their teams when events in the larger world were threatening lives and livelihoods.

Communicate clearly and consistently. The best recoveries from a crisis that we've seen came out of a leadership culture that was open and transparent: not just before the crisis, but during it, in the form of providing details in a timely, professional manner. Not only did this serve to assure staff that their leaders were competent and in control, it also helped shut down rumors and misinformation. As much as possible (and appropriate), be clear about what problems the organization is facing in light of the events, what you're doing to address them, and what your employees can expect from you. Be reassuring, but don't just say what you think people want to hear, or make promises you can't keep. If you're facing a shutdown, don't promise to keep paying salaries if you're not absolutely sure your finances can handle it for an unknown and possibly lengthy duration. People might understand being furloughed or laid off, but they will not understand or respect anyone who promises to take care of them and then fails to do so.

Change your operational practices to keep everyone safe. If being on site is dangerous, can your employees work from home? If they can and must work remotely, do they have reliable internet access? Are you able to equip and train them on laptops, routers, conferencing software, and so on? If your staff is in a rural area with poor internet access, can you cover their cellphone bills so they can hotspot? In our experience, the companies who are best positioned to survive a paradigm-shifting event are the ones who were flexible, and willing to accept quickly that they had to make changes to the way their staff worked.

Get ready to adapt—a lot. During the COVID-19 pandemic, many grocery stores were slow to respond due to conflicting information about, for instance, whether masks were effective at preventing spread. Store managers did find numerous ways to adapt, and as they learned more, they adapted more. They reduced their opening hours to allow more time for cleaning, disinfected shopping carts between uses, set out hand sanitizer stations, put arrows on the floor to direct traffic, installed Plexiglas shields at checkout points, put out floor markers to maintain distance in checkout lines, limited the number of customers who could be in the store, set aside shopping times for vulnerable shoppers, offered delivery and curbside pickup, and (eventually) required staff and customers to wear masks.

Don't let complexity stop you. Even big, sprawling enterprises can make the changes needed to provide physical and emotional safety to their customers—consider Shanghai Disney, which set up stations to check guests' temperature at the entrance to the park, presenting them with a health QR code (China's way of tracking the health of its people) to help them show that they had been cleared. Guests and cast members were required to wear masks at all times on property, except when eating. Shows, character interactions, and parades were suspended, advance reservation tickets were limited, and sanitation was increased. Staff and guests were not just *told* they were safe, they could see it and feel the precautions around them. Not sure if you're doing enough? Ask your people if they feel safe (or as safe as possible given the circumstances), then act on what they tell you.

Provide simple and specific directions. During chaotic times, your team needs to understand the exact direction of the company and of their contribution to it. The best recoveries we have seen involved spelling everything out clearly to staff members: hours of operation, dress codes, security procedures, flexibility to work from home, moving to part-time work, rotating shifts, logging hours, in-office childcare, and appropriate intervals for updating their supervisors on availability and completed tasks. Providing these details about expectations and flexibility removes unnecessary guesswork during a time when stress levels are high. When all hell is breaking loose, a bit of structure and clarity can be comforting. (At the same time, resist the urge to micromanage. Make your expectations known, then trust your people to do the best they can.)

Admit what you don't know. Sometimes a manager doesn't yet know how to respond to a specific situation. That's okay—it's unrealistic to expect everybody to know how to handle a new scenario, especially if they've never dealt with a large-scale disaster or prolonged crisis. But you need to be willing to *say* that you don't have a solution yet, while communicating that you're working on finding one. Act fast, yes, but act only on what you know to be true. If a natural disaster has occurred, what do trusted sources like NOAA, the Weather Channel, or your local news stations say? If another new virus has emerged, what do the scientists, doctors, and epidemiologists say? What safety precautions does the World Health Organization recommend? Predictions and recommendations change as more becomes known about the current threat; it might be a good idea to err on the side of caution and prepare for the worst-case scenario while hoping for the best. Avoid speculation and assumptions, as they will only fuel the crisis. Do your best with what you know, and when you know better, then do better.

Appoint a crisis management team. If you're running a large company, identify employees with leadership potential and get a team together to assist with communication and direction. This team could serve a variety of purposes: increasing morale, determining which departments are struggling with what, advocating for their colleagues, and using their day-to-day experience to suggest solutions and help higher management understand what immediate actions or changes could be most effective for the rank-and-file.

Check on your employees. A Mentor Manager is never afraid to pick up the phone. When the Pole Creek and Bald Mountain wildfires of central Utah merged into one rapidly spreading fire in September 2018, they burned more than

You need to be willing to share in the sacrifice that many employees are forced into.

120,000 acres and forced almost 6,000 people to evacuate. Ben Peterson and Ryan Sanders, the co-founders of BambooHR—located in Lindon, just north of the fire—personally called each of their employees who were affected by the fire. Ben and Ryan didn't send emails or text messages; they called.

Share in the sacrifice. As a leader—especially if you embrace the ideals of servant leadership set forth in this book—you need to be willing to share in the sacrifice that many employees are forced into. People who say they love where they work know that their managers will not ask anything of them that they aren't willing to do themselves. So follow that example. Do you need to cut your workers' salaries temporarily? Then cut your pay first, and cut it at least as much as you'll be cutting the pay of your employees, if not more. (Possibly a lot more, depending on how big the gap is between your pay and theirs.)

Evaluate, evaluate, evaluate. The companies we have worked with who have best survived downturns and crises have managers who are constantly evaluating what's working and what isn't. Not just during, but after: when a crisis ends, they conduct after-action reviews to learn what succeeded and what didn't, and prepare accordingly for the next crisis. Don't let the pain of the current situation happen for nothing; problems and crises are completely worthless if we don't learn from them.

Have patience and empathy. This is essential—you cannot expect things to function the way they used to when the current situation is nowhere near normal. Employees with children might suddenly have to be full-time teachers and caregivers at the same time as they're trying to keep up with the demands of their jobs. (This goes both ways: if you're also

struggling to home-school your kids while keeping your business running, your employees might need to exercise some patience with you too.) It's just science that prolonged stress can affect sleep, appetite, concentration, and mood, making a bad situation even more difficult.[1] Be a little more lenient with lateness, delays, or mistakes than you might otherwise be.

Above all, create hope. Nobody wants to follow a pessimist. In all my years of research, I have come to believe that successful CEOs and managers are optimists at heart. They have to be. Nobody knows how long any given crisis will last, nor do we know what life will look like on the other side. Loss is hard; uncertainty is hard. Your people need hope and a reason to hang in there long enough to get to that other side, even if "getting there" looks radically different than it did before. Share your belief that, eventually, with resourcefulness and determination, you'll find new ways to survive and thrive, and you *will* all get there.

Okay, Money *Does* Matter

Whether you're thinking about how to handle a crisis or wondering how to manage being more flexible in general, you'll have more options if your business is financially sound and you have a cushion. It can take time, effort, and restraint to get to that place, but if you *can* reach it, you and your employees will all breathe a little easier. You'll be better able to see your people as *people*, rather than as cogs in your industrial wheel. As Jeanette Bennett said to me:

> I can't have the mindset of "I'm trying to maximize every moment and every dollar"—even though, as a business owner, you *are* trying to maximize every moment, and every dollar. I can't feel that way about my people.

I asked Jeanette what helps her remember this mindset when business pressures are making it difficult, and while the response in her case was "I think some of it is innate in my soul," this ability also depends on two other, more universal factors that everyone can take some level of control over: culture and finances.

We've already discussed culture at length in previous chapters, so let's visit finances for a moment. Here's what Jeanette had to say about that topic:

> I think it comes down to sound business principles, because one of the things that allows me to not feel like I have to maximize every dollar and every hour is that my business has a cushion. I run my finances in such a way that alleviates the stress, and that's taken some self-discipline. I drove a dented minivan for eight years because I didn't want our company to have debt. I don't like to carry debt, because then you're a slave to it and you have to value money over people.

Again, not every company will always be able to operate without debt and with a cushion, but it's something to aim for. It will only give you greater stability, and a higher level of readiness for those inevitable rainy days.

But what if it's pouring right now? What if you're watching your bank account dwindle as a crisis stretches out? That means it's time to get creative. During the COVID-19 shutdown, some businesses survived by offering new services, or changing how they offered their products. Restaurants and cafés offered take-out food, with curbside pickup or delivery; some added grocery staples to their regular offerings. Professional organizers couldn't work in people's homes, so they offered virtual sessions and DIY plans. Personal trainers and yoga teachers offered classes online. Are there ways you could change your business model temporarily to help you weather the storm?

For the well-being of your people and the long-term success of your company, you need to prepare for when hard times hit—whether that's for your employee, your organization, your industry, or your whole country. You have a unique opportunity to instill hope, provide comfort, and remind your people what you stand for. Not only do they need to *be* safe, they also have to *feel* safe. Creating that sense of safety, both emotionally and professionally, is crucial because hard times reveal true character. After the crisis has passed, your people will remember how you responded to it.

MASTERING YOUR MOMENTS

Question #1: Do your employees know they can talk to you when they're going through a difficult time? If you answered yes, consider why you think this is true. Have people confided in you before? If you answered no, it's time to start making deposits of trust (see chapter four).

Question #2: How well is your company prepared for a crisis? Do you have a financial cushion, or a plan for reduced spending that could see you through an unexpected short-term crunch? What could you do to get flexible if your whole industry—or town, or country—is hit again with something as serious and out-of-the-blue as COVID-19?

Question #3: What have you done to make sure that your employees not only *are* safe from the possible impacts of a short- or longer-term crisis, but also *feel* safe? If you have a contingency plan for a crisis, have you communicated it? What could you do as a team to plan or prepare? Could you brainstorm ways to get creative together?

Challenge: Plan for hard times

If your organization weathered the COVID-19 pandemic, analyze what worked and what could have been done better. If you're leading a new organization (or one that's new to you), start scenario planning now for the next personal, local, or national crisis. How flexible are your sick leave and bereavement leave policies? What kinds of work could be done remotely? How well do you pay your employees? Is it enough so they can create cushions of their own? When someone needs help beyond what you can provide, do you have a network of professionals you can refer them to? Look at your financials; make a business continuity plan; run emergency drills; do whatever it takes to get as prepared as you can.

Surround yourself with astonishing people doing extraordinary things.

— 10 —

YOUR PERSONAL BOARD OF MENTORS

**It's what you learn after
you know it all that counts.**
JOHN WOODEN

S O MUCH of our perception and view of life comes from our environment, our culture, and the people we choose to associate with. This can be just as true in leadership and business: the world you've created around yourself is not only a reflection of the leader you will become, but also one of the biggest guiding factors in that development.

So far in this book we've discussed the effects that your influence, advocacy, and mentorship will have on the people you manage. But these same principles also apply to you and your relationship with your own mentors. And you are being mentored, whether you know it or not. Look around you: at your peers, at the managers and executives in the ranks above you, at the leaders who grab your attention in the media, in politics, in the books you read. Even if you are not consciously choosing these influences and role models, they are the people who are subtly affecting the way you understand and practice leadership.

As I've met and spoken with various CEOs and management teams during my undercover research, I've noticed one further ingredient that differentiates those leaders whose people "love it here" and those whose people don't. And that's making sure they have active, conscious mentorship. That's right—the great mentors were *always* being mentored. *Always*.

Consider these business leaders: Bill Gates of Microsoft, Larry Page and Eric Schmidt of Google, Shellye Archambeau of MetricStream, Sheryl Sandberg of Facebook, John Doerr of Kleiner Perkins, Emil Michael of Uber, Brad Smith of Intuit. They all had a mentor—and not just any mentor, the same mentor. His name was Bill Campbell, and they all called him "the coach." Eric Schmidt once said, "I think it should be the $2 trillion coach if you add it all up now... Everyone agrees they would not have been nearly as successful without that coaching."[1]

Campbell had originally played for—and later coached—Columbia University's football team. He then began working in various business industries, making a pit stop as the VP of marketing for Apple, and soon creating a reputation for himself as one of the premier mentors and advisors to some of the most profound and prominent leaders of our era.

This guidance didn't come when these leaders were young newbie managers. They were at the top of their game, and yet they still sought mentorship and advice. And if you look even closer at the magic behind their success, you'll often find that these executives didn't have just one coach—they had many.

Typically, a public company will have something called a board of directors. This group is made up of trusted advisors who have been elected by senior members of the company.

They can come from inside or outside the ranks, and they're primarily responsible for the oversight of the company's progress. They weigh in on major decisions, and bring advice, wisdom, and guidance. This board is key to keeping the company moving forward.

If *you* want to keep moving forward, you'll need your own kind of board of directors. Not a formal corporate board, with official roles and duties and a row of head shots listed in your annual prospectus. This is your *personal* board of directors—call it your "board of mentors." The people you choose for this board don't necessarily need to be affiliated with your company, nor would they have any legal or contractual authority over company decisions. They're simply a group of people, hand-selected by you, who you feel inspired by or want to emulate. These are the people who you turn to when you need advice, or who can provide you with a challenging or unique perspective that you can't see yourself.

Some of these mentors will gladly give you their time and guidance for free. Some may come at a cost. But you must be willing to make the investment—whether tangible or intangible—if you want to have control over the kind of leader you are becoming. You can't emulate that which you do not know. So surround yourself with astonishing people doing extraordinary things.

When I was young, my dad was my wrestling coach for over six years. He was a state champion wrestler himself and a master of the sport. He worked with me for countless hours to teach me the skills necessary to succeed. Every Friday night, my dad would take me to the local high school wrestling matches to watch the varsity team wrestle. Wasatch High School had one of the strongest programs in the state, with innumerable state championships, and it still produces some of the best wrestlers in the country.

Legendary wrestler Cael Sanderson—who is an Olympic gold medalist and the current head coach for Penn State University, one of the greatest wrestling programs in the country—was one of the high school wrestlers that I would watch. Week after week, we would make our way down to the school and watch Cael toss guys around the mat like rag dolls. Not only was he strong, he was also a very intelligent athlete. His ability to think and move around his opponent with precision and agility was always exciting to witness.

There were times I didn't want to go. Friday night is when kids kick back and hang out with friends, with no worries about school the next day. Sitting with my dad watching wrestlers was great and all, but not the only thing I wanted to do. One Friday, I asked my dad why we always went down to watch the high school team.

He said, "If you want to be a great wrestler, you've got to hang out by the mat."

As I've gotten older, I've come to realize the great value of this simple principle. If you want to be one of the greats, then hang out with the greats. Be where they are. Do what it takes to associate with the people who are the best at doing what you want to do. Start attending conventions and seminars. Reach out, ask questions, and stay curious. The relationship doesn't even have to be "in real life"—you're not always going be become friends with your heroes, but you can still learn from them: follow their Instagram accounts, join their Facebook groups, subscribe to their podcasts. Read their books, their blogs, and talk about what you learn with others. This can all put you on the road to finding your own network, and creating real relationships with people you trust and admire.

One of the most standout organizations I've had the opportunity to observe and research over the years is a real estate company known as Keller Williams. The company hosts a coaching program called MAPS, and the program's former CEO, Dianna Kokoszka, has earned a reputation as one of the most dynamic Mentor Managers in the industry, having led one of the top real estate training organizations in the world.

I can honestly say that nobody understands the value and worth of the idea that "great mentors are always being mentored" better than Dianna. Over the course of her tenure, she built a corporate-wide team of more than 370 accountability coaches. Over one year, the 5 percent of agents who had a coach for just seven weeks landed over 20 percent of the listings in the company while making 47 percent of all sales in the fourth quarter alone. That's an impressive amount of success from such a small percentage of people. Learning and associating with people who have walked the path before allows you to become part of that 5 percent.

So who are your coaches right now? Who is teaching and guiding you as you teach and guide those who work for you? (Whether that relationship is intentional or not!) Who are you consistently in contact with? Remember—you are influenced by the people you associate with most, and those you actively choose to learn from will have the greatest impact of all.

The "Five Cs" of Mentorship

As you think through the people in your life who you respect most in the search for potential mentors, don't measure them only by how much you like them or enjoy their company; rather, consider whether they have the qualities that make a good mentor. I call these the five Cs of mentorship:

1 They have confidence.
2 They have credibility.
3 They demonstrate competence.
4 They show candor.
5 They are caring.

Each one of these characteristics is essential in the people you choose as your mentors, because these are the characteristics you want others to find in *you* as a leader. Let's do a quick dive into what these characteristics look like in action, and the value they hold in both leadership and in the mentoring process.

1. Confidence

Confidence is a mindset. The Latin root *fidere* at the heart of the word means *to trust*. Does your mentor believe in themselves? Are they confident in the skills they're teaching? Are you confident in your own skills, and do you exude that confidence to your employees?

If you've ever seen *Shark Tank* or purchased anything from QVC, you know that Lori Greiner is the epitome of confidence—along with the other four Cs—and wildly successful in the business world. And rightfully so: she's an inventor and entrepreneur who has created over seven hundred products and owns over 120 patents. Her book *Invent It, Sell It, Bank It!* is a national bestseller, and she has an uncanny ability to know whether or not a product will be a winner. (Her success rate for product launches is over 90 percent.)

Do you think any of this success would have happened if Greiner did not have confidence in her own abilities? She has carried herself and her incredible team to exactly where she wants to be; she knows what she's good at, and she plays in that court. Do your existing or potential mentors have the same kind of confidence in their own abilities? Do they know

Can your mentor actually do what they are teaching you?

their strengths and play to them? Are they willing to bet on their abilities when no one else will? And what about yourself? How do you model confidence as a leader and mentor?

2. Credibility

Credibility is a person's résumé, their work history, and their experience. It's their schooling, their skills, their past jobs, their life experience. It's what qualifies them to train and mentor in a specific field or skill set. So, what qualifies your mentors? What do their résumés look like? Your mentors should be open to constantly improving their knowledge, skills, and experience to continually improve. And, of course, the same should stand for you.

Sidney Poitier has been an inspiration to many through his portrayals in films like *A Raisin in the Sun*, *Lilies of the Field*, and *Look Who's Coming to Dinner*. But what's most inspiring about him is his role as a mentor to up-and-coming actors. One such relationship was with Denzel Washington, who credits much of his success to Poitier's mentorship. On one occasion, Washington sought his advice on a major movie offer. It was an action flick, offering $600,000. The rate was unbelievable to the young actor at the time, but the movie had questionable messages on race. Poitier gave him sage council: "Son, your first three or four films will dictate how you are viewed in your entire career. Choose wisely, follow your gut and wait it out if you can."[2] Washington followed this advice and waited it out. The next year, he was offered a role in *Cry Freedom*, which won him his first Oscar nomination.

A credible mentor is someone who has "been there"— someone who has walked the walk and talked the talk, and will help you navigate your own journey.

3. Competence

While credibility is the knowledge and skill, competence is the actual application of that knowledge and skill. Your mentor may know everything about basketball—all the skills and statistics, rules and regulations—but do they actually play? Can they shoot the ball into the hoop? Can your mentor actually do what they are teaching you? Can you, in turn, actually do what you are teaching others?

Remember the Dream Team from chapter three? They wouldn't have come together as well as they did without the leadership of Chuck Daly. Not only did he know the sport, he also knew what it was like to be a star player, and to play alongside other star players. He had experience in dealing with ego and knew what it took to pull players together into a unified organism. That kind of competence can't come from reading guides and watching others, it can only come from doing. Look for the practitioner, not just the legend.

4. Candor

Candor is honesty. You need someone who can and will be completely and painfully honest with you. This is not the person who will constantly validate you or give you gold stars. You need someone who will give you honest and open feedback in all areas—even if it's uncomfortable—so that you can improve yourself.

Fearless, empathetic honesty is one of the most valuable things you can receive from a mentor. Everyone needs someone who they can trust to be candid with them, especially in areas of improvement. And having someone in your life who can do this for you will teach you how to be that same person for those you mentor.

Brad Stevens, head coach of the Boston Celtics, is a great model for this kind of candor. Describing his style of coaching, Zach Lowe of ESPN once said, "He focuses on actions: *We didn't get this rebound. You should have made this rotation earlier.* The criticism is never about the player's character. No one is labeled lazy or stupid or selfish. Stevens simply describes what did or did not happen, and what should happen next time."[3]

Building the type of candid rapport that Brad Stevens has with his players takes time and attention. It takes a kind of trust that develops when you know that the feedback you receive from your coach is for your benefit and not just to air grievances and disappointments. When you find this in a mentor, you can model it to your staff: that kind of a relationship will build an atmosphere of honesty and respect over time.

Fearless, empathetic honesty is one of the most valuable things you can receive from a mentor.

---

5. Caring

If there is no connection, it's nearly impossible for mentoring to take place. You need to find someone who cares, who values you as a person, and who really wants you to succeed. You need someone who is willing to go to bat for you, just as you need to be willing to go to bat for your people. Does your mentor value you as a person, and do they have your best interests at heart? Are they happier when they see you succeed?

In the Undercover Millennial program, we've done a fair amount of research in the educational space, going in to talk with students and staff at universities and college campuses. As I did this research myself at one particular college—walking around campus, conversing with students and staff in various departments, asking things like "What's it like going to college here?" "Do you like teaching here?" or "What's the campus like?"—an obvious and consistent trend I noticed among the answers was the name Robert Houlihan, or, as he was called affectionately, Bob. Everybody had a story about Bob, and how Bob had changed their life in one way or another—and I mean *everybody*.

Through several conversations, I learned that Bob had been at Molloy College for thirty-six years, starting as the softball coach and eventually coaching six All-American players and winning the ECAC Championships in 1994 and 1995. By the end of his time at Molloy, he had worked his way to becoming vice president of student affairs. In 2017, he retired after a lifetime of service to his students.

After witnessing this collective fervor for Bob, I thought, "I have to meet him before I fly out!" Bob was gracious enough to sit down with me, but not before offering me a box of cherry-filled donuts. I happily accepted as he said, "I thought you might enjoy one as we talk."

I told Bob I was honored to meet him, and that everybody on campus seemed to have a story about him. He laughed and said, "Well, it's not about me."

That selflessness, I thought, is exactly why everyone has a story about him.

Bob and I spent quite a while talking about his time at Molloy, his personal beliefs, and his ideas on life and leadership. He didn't see the students as freshmen or seniors, athletes or thespians, or even groups of specific majors. "Everybody is somebody, somewhere, and it's my job to make sure they're a somebody here," he said. He told me about the responsibility he felt as a steward over the staff and the students, who often called him "coach" or "boss." He believed in catching people doing good, and that everybody had a story to tell. It was the highlight of his career to advocate for his students and to help them tell their story better. Bob is the type of person who dedicates his entire life to helping other people achieve their dreams. Even though he's retired now, I believe he will never be truly replaced—simply because he cared.

This is the kind of mentor who propels people forward. Find your Bob; someone to help you go where you want to go, and be that kind of mentor for your own employees. The moment you stop caring about a person you have stewardship over is the moment you both fail. Help them become more, while you strive to become more yourself.

IF YOU look on the other side of this coin, there is one more C to consider: callousness. While a good mentor will always propel you forward, I have also seen in my research how easy it is for an emerging leader with great potential to start adopting toxic behaviors in their management because they've chosen to listen to other managers who don't care about the people they lead.

Take a moment and ask yourself: Who are the loudest voices around you? Are you surrounding yourself with people who are constantly complaining, only seeing the negative, and never seeing what's right? Do your peers or influences use bad habits or manipulative tactics to create quick results? It might be time to change the balance by bringing new people into your life, or even exiting those relationships.

Keep in mind, however: character matters, and reputation matters—yours, as well as theirs. If it's time to leave a mentorship situation (whether that's due to toxicity, a bad fit, or even a helpful relationship that's run its course), make sure that even the most difficult of conversations is held with the utmost respect and care. *Always.* You can't forget that you sought them out in the first place. Acknowledge the help and any growth or accomplishments you've achieved with their guidance, and say "thank you." Gratitude will always win.

Be Teachable

What happens if you have the right mentors, but you find you still aren't making any progress? "You can't teach an old dog new tricks," they say—but the truth is, age has nothing to do with it. Your ability (or inability) to learn has everything to do with your mindset: if you're afraid of change or new ideas because it threatens your idea of your expertise and what you think you already know, it will be difficult, if not impossible, to persuade you to change your opinions and behavior patterns.

The world and our understanding of it is constantly evolving, and we need to recognize that there are things we do not know. Being teachable allows us to accept those things, learn, and graciously apply what we've learned to our personal and professional lives.

Okay, when I say age has *nothing* to do with it, that's not always the whole truth. Oftentimes, people remain stuck and unteachable because they struggle to take direction from someone who's younger than them. This is a damaging way to look at the mentoring relationship. Age should have zero impact on who you choose as your mentors. If you put aside your biases, you'll see that some of the most qualified people to help guide you might be younger than you.

No matter what your generation is, the people coming up behind you will have a fresher perspective and a natural understanding of the world, both as it is now and as it's becoming. And, it must be said, similar is true of generations that are older than you—they have a perspective on life and business that can only be earned with experience. Having a mix of age groups within your personal board of mentors will let you tap into the value of each of these perspectives: "greatest" and "silent" generations, baby boomers, Gen X, Gen Z, and whoever is coming over the horizon next.

The most successful leaders share a unique strength that comes from the ability to stay in what Liz Wiseman, author of *Rookie Smarts*, refers to as "rookie mode." This is when you can acknowledge that you may not be the most experienced person in a specific area, and you are willing to remain humble and receive counsel from other sources. These sources could be business owners who are ahead of you, financial advisors who are younger than you, or somebody who is simply better than you at what you do. The more you learn, the more you understand how much you don't actually know. The greatest managers allow themselves to exist in that challenging space.

As you grow in your position as a person of influence within your organization, you're going to have rough days. You'll be bombarded with various opinions explaining why you should not do *this*, or why you should do *that*. These comments will come not only from other leaders, but also from your employees. Having your personal board of mentors will help you keep focused amidst the distractions and people who may or may not have your best interests at heart. They will help you keep *the main thing the main thing*, and turn your gaze back to the bigger picture, even in the face of criticism or short-term failure.

We all have days when we need to lean on someone—and that doesn't just go for you, it goes for your employees as well. When you have great mentors to lean on, you will be in a better position to become a great mentor for someone else.

MASTERING YOUR MOMENTS

Question #1: Look around you: Who are you learning from, whether you have thought of them as formal mentors or not? How have they affected the way you lead?

Question #2: What would your ideal board of mentors look like? How could you start developing relationships with the people you want to learn from?

Question #3: How do you exemplify the five Cs of mentorship with your own employee mentoring?

Challenge: Create your board of mentors
Make a list of five people who might make a good mentor to you. List their characteristics and talents and compare them against the five characteristics of a good mentor (the "five Cs"), as well as what you're personally looking for in a mentor. Reach out to at least three people on your list and ask them what it would take to have them as your mentor. Choose at least one person on the list to actively mentor you in your business or personal life.

We don't realize the importance of **having a sense of purpose** until it is suddenly taken from us.

HELPING THEM LIVE, NOT JUST EXIST

To live is the rarest thing in the world. Most people exist, that is all.

OSCAR WILDE

LET ME share one more string of memories with you—it starts on an airplane and ends at the biggest crossroads I have ever faced. I was sitting in the cockpit of a single-engine DA20 Katana. I had this big ol' headset on, and I was on the taxiway, getting ready to pull onto runway 3-1. With one hand, I grabbed the joystick in front of me, and with the other I punched the button to declare over the radio, "Heber City Traffic—this is Katana 1-0-6 Whiskey Alpha, taking the active runway 3-1. Any traffic in the area, please advise. Heber City Traffic."

Over the loud hum of the engine, I strained to listen for any other aircraft in the traffic pattern. I heard nothing but the engine. The runway was mine.

I eased up off the brakes, gave the throttle just a little bit of juice, and pushed the left rudder pedal so I could align my airplane with that mile-long strip of asphalt. The propellor was spinning, and the wind conditions were absolutely perfect. As I sat on the centerline, the theme song from *Top Gun* began playing in my head. I shoved the throttle forward as far as it could go. The plane jumped from 20 knots to 30, then 40 knots, then 50 knots. As I eased back on the stick, the front wheel sputtered. The plane tilted back, and the drag of the back two wheels became softer and softer and softer—until 3 . . . 2 . . . 1 . . . liftoff.

I was flying with the birds.

I was eighteen, a senior in high school who barely knew how to drive a car, and I was flying a plane. The coolest part about this whole experience was that, when I looked over at the seat next to me, nobody was there.

That was the day I took my first solo flight.

If you ask any pilot to talk about the day they first soloed, they'll be able to tell you every single detail—the weather, the plane, the time, what they were wearing, everything. You don't forget moments like that. I was on cloud nine, and literally flying full speed in the direction of my destiny. This is what I wanted to do with the rest of my life. Hanging from my bedroom ceiling was every toy helicopter and toy airplane ever sold at Toys R Us, alongside the aviation toys my mom and I scavenged from garage sales. I ate, slept, and drank aviation. I was going to grow up to be a Life Flight helicopter pilot. There was nothing more exhilarating than the thought of flying a turbine helicopter up to a mountain to drop a paramedic out the side to rescue some stranded climber.

That's what I wanted to do, and I was well on my way to achieving it. By the time I graduated from high school, I had my pilot's license. That certificate meant more to me than my high school diploma.

Shortly after I graduated, I served a two-year mission for my church. When I returned home, I had to renew my driver's license. We've all had the blessed experience of the DMV. It's horrible—there are so many lines, like Disneyland in the summertime, but with no Mickey or churros. On the day I went, I waited an hour and a half just for my number to be called.

"Number 242 at kiosk four. Number 242."

Finally. Jumping from my chair, I walked up to the counter and set my paperwork down. The lady immediately started flipping through my paperwork. She didn't look at me or say a word. Self-checkout lines are more cordial.

"Uh huh," she said as she glanced over the paper. "Yup. Okay..." She scribbled something on the front page, then gestured to a black box at the side of the counter. I hesitated, not knowing what I was supposed to do. She just glared, waiting, until she realized that I was oblivious to the significance of the box. "Go ahead," she demanded, as if her insistence would clarify things. I stepped toward the box, then looked back at her with the same vacant expression. Rolling her eyes, she added, "Stick your head in the box."

I did as she said and pressed my head into the opening.

"Click the button on the side and tell me what you see," she said. "Make sure you push hard."

I pressed my head harder against the box, squinting as I clicked the button. The screen went white, showing six black dots.

Click. Still only six black dots. I looked up and said, "Ma'am, I don't know if this is working."

"Did you make sure you push hard?" she demanded.

I tried again. Click. Nothing. Just the pale illumination of the back-panel light showing six faint dots.

"Ma'am, it's not working. Can I try a different box?"

She slowly looked up from the paperwork and said, "I've been here for eight hours today. I've already seen dozens of people, and every single one of them has put their head in that same black box and read the letters. Now *read the letters!*"

Frustration boiled up from inside. Straining to keep it in, I clenched my fist and gritted my teeth. I didn't want a scene; I just wanted my driver's license and to be on my way. I stepped to the box again.

Click.

Click.

Click. Click. Click. I began jabbing the button *repeatedly* in complete agitation. Still nothing.

She pushed the paperwork aside, stood, and stomped her way around the counter. Pushing me out of the way, she put her head in the device and called out, "C-K-G-E-L-F-Z-Y." Turning from the box to me, she looked at me as if I were an imbecile. "I can read the letters," she said. "I just need *you* to read them." She stepped aside to give me space.

I glanced into the box. Still nothing. "Look, I don't see anything."

We stared at each other until her anger slowly faded to realization. "Honey," she said. "I think you're blind."

"What are you talking about?" I scoffed. "I drove here."

"Well, you ain't driving back." She reached over the counter for a big red stamp and with a decisive slam stamped my paperwork. In large red letters, it read: "Driving Privileges Denied: Did Not Pass Vision Test."

With no driver's license and unable to leave the DMV on my own, I had to call my mother. "Mom," I said, "I'm going to need a ride home."

"A ride?" she asked, confused. "Why?"

I took a deep breath. It didn't really hit me until that moment what it all meant. "Mom," I replied. "I'm blind."

Long story short, I ended up at the Moran Eye Center at the University of Utah, where one of the leading authorities diagnosed me with a rare eye disease known as keratoconus. Because the disease is degenerative, my eyesight would progressively get worse as I grew older. Over time, my corneas would get thinner and thinner and thinner, until eventually I would go completely blind. Back then, there were only two ways to handle this disease: allow it to progress, or receive cornea transplants.

As I said in the very first chapter, I firmly believe that a single moment in time can change a person's life. Learning that my eyesight would deteriorate was one such moment. I sat there in that white room and listened to the doctor tell me the chances were that I would be blind for the rest of my life.

"Your eyes are about as bad as an eighty-seven-year-old's," the doctor said. "By the time you are between age thirty or thirty-four, you'll be blind." Then he asked, "What do you want to do for a living? What do you want to do when you grow up? What's your plan for a career?"

"I want to fly," I said. "I want to be a pilot."

The doctor looked at me solemnly. "Not anymore," he said. "With your condition, you should never, nor will you ever, be in a cockpit."

A few years later I was lucky enough to be in the very first clinical trial for a new procedure called "corneal cross-linking." I had the procedure done in 2012, first on my right eye and then, four months later, on my left. It stopped the degeneration 100 percent—cross-linking worked, and it was fully approved by the FDA in 2016. But in that doctor's office on the day I was diagnosed, there was as yet no cure. One minute I was a young person with purpose, direction, and my eye on the sky; the next minute I saw that sky come crashing down around me.

The lesson has stayed with me, even if the threat of blindness did not: we don't realize the importance of having a sense of purpose until it is suddenly taken from us.

Being the Best for the World

One of the most significant things I have witnessed in my experience with the Undercover Millennial program is the number of employees who are merely existing, who have no purpose. They have forgotten the value of living, especially in their work environments, and their jobs have become just paychecks to them. Because of this, they have no loyalty to the company they work for, and there is nothing keeping them from jumping ship as soon as something better comes along.

What they lack is direction and a reason to stay. But as I have said throughout this book, the true value of my experience with this program has come in the lessons I learn from the employees who love their jobs and are living authentically within them—because they have leaders who care, and who connect them to something bigger. It is these Mentor Managers who make all the difference. By now, I hope that you've been able to internalize the point that every successful thing these managers do comes back to having a greater focus on their people. They never forget that *what you do* and *why you do it* should always be built on a foundation of authentic care and genuine connection—creating a legacy along with the change.

I've spent a lot of time mentoring and working with teenagers and high school students, helping them see the bigger picture and gain a better understanding of how they can contribute to society in a way that's important and meaningful to them. When I ask them what they want to do with their life, the answer that I most often get is "I don't know." It's not surprising that many young people don't yet know what kind of work they want to do or what matters most to them. After all, it usually takes time, experience, and experimentation to figure that out.

What's troubling is that so many people don't seem to figure it out—*ever*. According to a 2017 Gallup survey, 85 percent of working adults in the U.S. hate their jobs, which means that only 15 percent are happily engaged in the direction of their lives.[1] But let's not focus on the 85 percent who are unhappy; let's shift our attention to the 15 percent who love what they do. How were they able to figure it out and find meaning, joy, and fulfillment in their work?

Early in our interviews, we were surprised to find that one of the primary reasons people love their jobs isn't because of the tangible benefits, like great pay, great insurance, location, or other perks (though those factors certainly help). It's because they find fulfillment within the intangibles: joy, passion, excitement, energy, a sense of purpose, a feeling of belonging, the feeling that they matter. So, we began asking how and why this is the case.

The findings that came from this analysis weren't a surprise, but a reiteration of something I have always believed to be true. We discovered that the number one factor behind an employee finding purpose and fulfillment in their job is association and connection with other purposeful and fulfilled people.

This is where you come in.

Even before the massive upheaval caused by the COVID-19 pandemic, the Pew Research Center found that employees were experiencing major uncertainty regarding their economic, political, and professional futures. Pew reported that about half of American parents do not believe that their children will be better off than they were.[2] Millennials and Gen Zs are scared—and many are rudderless. The biggest problem in the workplace today is not actually stress, lack of benefits, or being overworked—it's feeling meaningless.

Young employees especially are looking to business leaders to provide ethics and passion and to help them see where they fit into the bigger picture. They're begging for meaningful work, and begging to associate with other remarkable people. When they aren't able to find that in their current position, they're moving on to other jobs and—more importantly—other managers.

One of my favorite movies of all time (almost ranking with *Top Gun*) is *The Sandlot*. Now a cult classic, the film follows a boy named Scotty Smalls who moves to a new neighborhood and makes friends with a group of kids who play baseball at the nearby sandlot. Together they go on a series of funny and touching adventures, and eventually run into trouble when Scotty secretly borrows his dad's baseball, signed by the legendary Babe Ruth. The ball gets knocked over a fence, into a yard guarded by an enormous and vicious dog known as "the Beast." Calamity ensues as the kids try to retrieve the ball from their canine adversary.

During this adventure, one of the boys, named Benny, has a dream in which Babe Ruth appears to him and gives him advice on how to get the ball back. Right before Babe departs, he turns to Benny and says, "Remember, kid, heroes get remembered, but legends never die."

Remember my old teacher Mr. Jensen, who gave me the drumsticks? Every time I watch that movie and hear that line, I think of him, because the memory of what he did for me will never die. I prefer to think of the line as: "Heroes get remembered, but Mr. Jensens never die."

Heroes get
remembered, but
**Mr. Jensens
never die**.

If you think this is an exaggeration, consider this (and keep your phone in your pocket): who were the last three NFL MVPs? What were their names, and what teams did they play on? Do you know? Let's try another question. Who were the last two Academy Award winners for Best Actor or Actress? Or the names of the last two winners of the Miss America pageant? Nothing? Perhaps business would be easier. What two companies had the highest profit margins last year? Still nothing? Don't feel bad. Most people are unable to come up with the right answers.

Now try this: think of an educator or mentor who made a difference in your life. Do you remember their name? Tell me who your best friend was growing up, or the name of a person who was there for you during a difficult time. Tell me the name of a co-worker who made your work life more enjoyable.

But wait—before you answer, consider this: when I asked you to name some of the richest, most athletic, most talented, most beautiful individuals who exist, you found that you could maybe name one, but it's unlikely that you knew all of them. But now I've asked about the mentors and others who created significance in your life, and I bet you remember not only the name, but several moments associated with that person too. I even bet you could tell me each way they added significant value to your life.

Why were you able to do that? It's because of their importance to you. It's because they were the people who understood that it's always about the person. They were the ones who took the time to see you as an individual with needs. And for that, they will always stay alive in your mind. Because heroes get remembered, but Mr. Jensens never die.

If you've ever read a deathbed study, you'll know how fascinating it is to hear what people have to say in their last moments. It's amazing what you can learn about life by studying death. Nobody ever says they wish they'd made more money or lived in a bigger house. Nobody ever wishes they'd worked more hours at the office or moved higher up the corporate ladder. Instead, people express their desire to have had better relationships with those in their lives. They wished they'd spent more time with their parents, had been a better friend, or taken care of the people who were really in need. They wished they could have made more meaningful connections with the people they loved most.

Not only did they regret the lack of meaningful connections, they also regretted not contributing to something bigger than themselves. They yearned for fulfillment of purpose during their journey—they wished they had stopped trying to be the best *in* the world, and instead focused more on being the best *for* the world.

Purpose, Passion, and the Ability to Provide

Mark Twain said, "There are two important days in a person's life—the day you are born and the day that you figure out why." When you figure out why, and you have the opportunity to be a part of that on a daily basis, then you are opening the doors to living your best life. You get a chance to dream, not just work. I believe that to live means to find fulfillment, to know happiness, and to realize significance. To live is to be filled with passion—and to feel like you're a part of something bigger than yourself. When you're living like that, you feel like you're doing your best work and making a significant contribution to the world around you.

In flight school, I had learned the importance of keeping a heading and maintaining your navigational course. After I discovered my corneal blindness and my dream of flying was over, I felt directionless. How do you keep a heading when you don't have a defined destination? In desperation, I set my sights on college. After all, isn't that the next step after high school? My father was in the medical profession and seemed to enjoy it well enough, so I decided it could also be the right profession for me.

I buried my passion for flying and ended up going to college to get my undergraduate degree. I decided to visit one of the school's career counselors, Kirk Young, to get some direction. I had heard that the medical field was a great career to go into, but wanted some guidance to ease my hesitations. I had never been strong in math and I was afraid that I wouldn't be able to adequately complete the math requirement to excel in the medical field.

Kirk greeted me warmly at the door to his office. After we shook hands and exchanged names, he ushered me in.

"Have a seat," he said, offering me a chair near the desk.

I thanked him and sat down. After I was settled, he leaned forward attentively. "How can I help you?" he asked.

"I'm trying to decide what major to go into," I replied. "Right now, I'm thinking about the medical program."

He nodded as he listened. "Do you have questions about the program?" he asked.

"Kind of," I said. Every time I discussed the medical field, I felt no passion. Sure, everyone was impressed with the decision, but it wasn't like aviation. I couldn't stop talking about aviation, but with the medical field, I couldn't wait to be done talking about it. It usually entered conversations right after the topic of college came up, generally with uncles or aunts, and occasionally complete strangers. They would all ask the same question: "What are you studying?" I would say medicine or the medical field, and they would all say what a great profession it was. But somehow, deep down, I didn't feel the same way. So I would just change the topic.

"I'm afraid I may not be able to complete the math requirements," I told the counselor.

He studied me as if he knew there was something else to my reservations about the program. "I'm sure with the right effort, you will do just fine. But let me ask you a question. If you could do anything with no worry of money or anything else, what would you do?"

I shifted in my chair, squirming to find a comfortable position. The question had made me uncomfortable, because it hit a very sore spot with me. Even though I had forced all that passion down deep inside, it yearned to get out. It was like imprisoning everything I was—my very soul. I would never do that to anyone else, but here I was doing it to myself. Perhaps it was that weight of conscience that made the question uncomfortable. It was like I was under one of those interrogation lamps you see in the movies, and I had just been asked where I was on the night my passion was murdered.

"I don't know," I said shrugging.

Unsatisfied with my response, Kirk shifted back in his chair with his hands pressed together at the fingertips, carefully knitting together his next words. "There is a quote that I have found quite profound in life and I would like you to consider it. It comes from the Irish playwright Oscar Wilde. He said, 'To live is the rarest thing in the world. Most people exist, that is all.'"

Straightening, he looked me in the eyes. "The profession you choose will have a profound impact on your life. It will, in a large part, determine whether you just exist or whether you live."

I chuckled nervously. "Well, I want to live, of course," I said with a degree of disregard. After all, it's just a saying, right? "The medical field is a great profession," I tried to convince myself silently. "Anyway, it wasn't my choice to develop an eye disease that threw my life plans off course. I had my fun with aviation and now it's over. It's time for that passion to be put to better use."

We spent the rest of the time discussing the possibilities of the medical field. Kirk also pointed me in the direction of the leadership program at the university, which I entered. It was there that I was introduced to people like Stephen Covey and Joseph Grenny, who came to speak about success and leadership. There was something about the way they talked and the sense of excitement that came after hearing them that kept drawing me back.

During my undergraduate experience, I was lucky enough to become a presidential leader in the Center for the Advancement of Leadership, as well as orientation director, UVU ambassador, and UVU student body vice president—all roles that I loved. I loved the leadership program, too, but I didn't know what I could do with it. In the end, I went in the direction of medicine and became an orthopedic consultant.

With my new profession, I was able to buy a car, build a house, and enjoy life's luxuries. All my ducks were in a row. I had a good education and what many people would consider a good job, making lots of money. Still, that quote haunted me:

To live is the rarest thing in the world.

I couldn't shake it. I knew that something was missing, but I didn't know what to do about it. You can't have a bearing without a destination, and I had no destination.

My thoughts continually drifted back to the quote. Every day as I rose to go to work, a pricking in my heart told me this is not what I was supposed to be doing. There was something more out there for me. I reflected on those speakers I had listened to during the leadership program. They were energetic and filled with a fervor for what they taught. They were living, and they were inspiring others to do the same.

One day, while two friends and I were eating lunch at our favorite burger joint, we began talking about life. We were all pretty successful from the world's point of view, but we felt no enthusiasm about what we did. It was in the middle of discussing our professional lives that I dropped the bomb—the very same one that the counselor had dropped on me in his office. Only now, I added three criteria.

"What if you could have a job that did three things?" I asked. "One, it allowed you to do what you love, where you end the day fulfilled, not just tired. Two, it completely provided for your financial needs, and three, it allowed you to do something bigger than yourself—something that contributed to your purpose."

My friends looked at me with the same expression that I must have had in that counselor's office.

"Doesn't exist," one of my friends exclaimed. "There is no such job that will give you all that."

"Why not?" I demanded.

"Just think about it," said my other friend. "A teacher may love teaching and he is fulfilling something bigger than himself, but he is dirt poor. Most have to work through the summer just to make ends meet."

"And then there's doctors," added the first friend. "They do a great service and can make a decent wage, but are constantly overworked and stressed out, never seeing their families, and completely bogged down with lawsuits." He shook his hand, brushing aside the notion. "Doesn't exist."

I sat back in the booth, disheartened. Purpose, passion, and the ability to provide—for yourself, and for the people who are dependent on you. Twirling a fry in sauce, I wondered if maybe such a job *didn't* exist. If I still had the opportunity to be an aviator, there was no guarantee that I would have all three of those things either. Sure, I would

I wasn't a pilot. I was an explorer, and I realized that it's **okay to not have a clear destination**.

be doing something I love, but would I be fulfilling a higher purpose? Certainly the pay would not be as good. I would also be away from my family a lot. Many aspects of the career might not have worked out well even if I'd been able to stay in aviation. Then the thought came.

Living is a rare thing.

I looked up from the now saturated fry. "What if such a job *did* exist? Sure it may be rare, but what if it's out there waiting for us. Shouldn't we at least try looking for it?"

My friends glanced at each other skeptically. They both shrugged, just as I had in the counselor's office.

This time, however, I was not so dismissive. Two weeks later, I quit my job as an orthopedic consultant. I may not have had a clear destination, but I finally had a general bearing. Flight school taught me to be a pilot, but I wasn't a pilot. I was an explorer, and I realized that it's okay to not have a clear destination. It was a leap of faith that somewhere out there, in the unexplored regions of my life, was that passion I once had.

The next few years were not easy. I pursued the career of professional speaking, and in the process I developed the Undercover Millennial program. Through that program, I found individuals who, like me, had great jobs—but were miserable. I also found others who had seemingly miserable jobs, but loved them because of bosses who were authentic in their leadership. These inspiring men and women had made their companies truly rare. They were anomalies, but were utilizing principles that could be adopted by other businesses to create similar successes.

By applying these principles, these innovative influencers created an environment where people didn't just exist—they thrived. These leaders took it upon themselves to direct their employees in the fulfillment of those three criteria that I had presented to my friends:

- They brought out their employees' strengths and passions in the work they did.

- They listened to the needs of their employees and did what they could to meet those needs. This includes paying employees well and fairly so they can provide for their families.

- They gave them a clear vision of something bigger than themselves, and provided a sense of purpose.

The Undercover Millennial program has taught me that, by ensuring these three areas are satisfied in their employees, successful Mentor Managers provide a work environment that's a joy to be a part of. They create an environment where their employees find joy in living too—even as they work. As you apply these principles in your business, you will see the same results.

The day I left my job as an orthopedic consultant was the day I started living. It was one of the greatest decisions of my life. (At the time, I had house and car payments and other expenses, so even with a little bit of money in my savings, the jump still felt risky.) You likely have employees in your company who feel as lost as I did. They may feel as my friends did, that no job exists that can fulfill the three criteria. It is definitely rare. But it doesn't have to be. As an employer, you have the ability to create such a place for your own employees. This kind of environment is made up of small, seemingly insignificant moments that will inspire your people to start living true to who they are.

As a Mentor Manager, you have both the privilege and the opportunity to help your employees live better lives—a life with passion, with purpose, and, yes, with the ability to provide for their needs. These "three Ps" are for us as managers too: we each are given moments that offer a chance to take up the call to live instead of merely existing. These moments are different for each of us, but we all have them, and they are almost always initiated by a mentor who sees our potential.

It's not just about getting your employees to say "I love it here." It's also about getting them to say "I love who I am while I'm here." You can create that kind of appeal, that kind of workplace, that kind of culture. By building an environment where your employees can envision themselves as not just the best *in* the world, but also the best *for* the world, you can foster a mindset for your people that will inspire them to find their own path toward truly living.

MASTERING YOUR MOMENTS

Question #1: How has implementing the challenges in this book helped you to create more meaningful moments with those in your sphere of influence?

Question #2: How have you changed as a result of the challenges presented in this book?

Question #3: How can you continue to create meaningful moments in both your personal and professional life?

Challenge: Just do it

If you have not taken up the challenges in this book, go back to the end of each chapter, answer the questions, and accept the challenges. Knowledge is power, but only if you use it. I promise you that if you apply the principles of this book to your personal and professional life, you will have deeper, more meaningful relationships with those around you, and especially with those you lead. If you *have* applied the challenges, come back to this book often and repeat them. Each time you do, it will be a new experience because you will be at a different place. Your answers will change as you continue to grow and develop, and your application will be even more effective. If you continually apply these principles and practices to your life and your business, your company will thrive because your employees are thriving. And when asked about their job, they will eagerly say, "I love it here!"

We're trying to
master **mentorship as
a way of being**,
not just as a title.

— 12 —

SMALL THINGS OVER A LONG PERIOD OF TIME

**Greatness does not come from a function
of circumstance. Greatness comes from
a function of conscious choice and discipline.**
JIM COLLINS

THIS MAY BE the end of the book, but it's also, I hope, the beginning of a long and fulfilling process. While striving to be the mentor that your employees need you to be, it's important to remember that Rome wasn't built in a day. In fact, it took exactly 1,009,491 days. That's roughly 2,765 years.

The eleven principles I have described here are effective, but implementing them will not yield *immediate* results. Mentorship is a journey, not a destination. Like art, it must be molded, reformed, and rethought. Artists know that they must always be willing to change in order to create. Pilots know that it's one thing to follow a flight plan, but another to continually react to changing conditions. As a drummer, I know that I can't just follow a musical chart, I have to

internalize the music and let it work through me. We're trying to master mentorship as a way of being, not just as a title.

"So how much time does it take?" you may be asking.
"How do I know it will pay off?" With so much responsibility
to embody, you may even be wondering: "How do I implement all this without losing my mind?"

In 2015, my friend James Lawrence, also known as "The
Iron Cowboy," set out to do the unthinkable: complete fifty
triathlons, in fifty days, in fifty different states. That's 2.4 miles
of swimming, 112 miles of cycling, and a full 26.2-mile marathon *every single day for fifty days consecutively*, while traveling
through the U.S. It's quite possibly one of the most remarkable physical feats ever performed.

I've known James for several years now, and I've had the
opportunity to speak and share the stage with him on a few
occasions. As he presents he always interacts with his audience, and, without fail, the biggest question he receives is:
"How?" How did he prepare, execute, and, above all, swim,
bike, run, and maintain the physical and mental stamina to be
able finish fifty Ironmans in fifty states in fifty days?

His answer is always the same.

"I did small things, consistently, over a long period of time.
That's it. Small things, consistently, over a long period of time."

This concept of doing small things is profound, especially when it comes to learning mentorship, and mentoring
others. The magic is not in the amount of time you put in,
but in the consistent effort: a few minutes a day to give a
word of encouragement, a simple email with a few authentic
strategies that have helped you, or maybe some quick but
insightful feedback on a recent project. If your attitude is
always focused on mentoring your employees toward greater
success, and not just managing them, these small opportunities will arise. And just like my friend The Iron Cowboy,

you'll find that those brief yet profound moments will build into something remarkable. In your case, becoming a Mentor Manager to your employees.

I'm not here to tell you that mentorship is easy, because it isn't. It's not a simple checklist to success. Mentorship is a craft that takes conscious effort and consistent dedication. As you can witness in any marathon runner, body builder, elite dancer, or veteran musician, excellence stems from the rituals we put in place in order to improve.

There's an old saying that goes, "The faintest ink is more powerful than the strongest memory." You're going to slip into old habits, fail at new strategies, make mistakes, and even sometimes forget what you've learned. Keeping a written record of what works—and what doesn't—will help you stay on track in your growth as a leader. Think of this as your "mentorship cookbook." Write down your successes, and moments that made you and your employees feel energized and hopeful. Record the times that a tactic didn't work as well as you'd hoped. Learn from your successes, and from your mistakes. This simple practice will also give you the ability to reference and remember what worked, and why.

Let me give you an example. Thomas Edison was one of the greatest scientific inventors of our time. More patents were given to him than anyone else in U.S. history, totaling 1,093.[1] His inventions changed our world, including the motion picture camera, the phonograph, the light bulb, and telephone communication. Edison's productivity far exceeded that of any other scientist and inventor of his time. And in order to keep up on his inventions and experiments, Edison kept detailed journals of every experiment, idea, business dealing, patent, and future inventions.

In these journals he detailed not only his successes, but also his failures. During his work on the light bulb, Edison

The greatest part about
your role in leadership
is that it matters.
**The hardest part is that
it matters every day**.

went through hundreds of possible filaments, each failing until he stumbled on the carbonized cotton filament. Although many of Edison's attempts led to failures, this didn't stop him. During an interview with B.C. Forbes, Edison said:[2]

> I never allow myself to become discouraged under any circumstances. I recall that after we had conducted thousands of experiments on a certain project without solving the problem, one of my associates, after we had conducted the crowning experiment and it had proved a failure, expressed discouragement and disgust over our having failed "to find out anything." I cheerily assured him that we had learned something. For we had learned for a certainty that the thing couldn't be done that way, and that we would have to try some other way. We sometimes learn a lot from our failures if we have put into the effort the best thought and work we are capable of.

This same mentality has driven many others to succeed. When NASA endeavored to send a man to the moon, they had many setbacks—one that even resulted in the death of three astronauts. Still, they continued, learning from their failures and documenting their successes. In the end, you get where you want to go, even if it's hundreds of thousands of miles away.

The most successful leaders we've worked with in the Undercover Millennial program practice all of the principles you have found in this book, and they practice them on a constant, consistent basis. They understand all of this:

1 A single moment in time is priceless, and can change a person's direction in life.

2 Leadership is a key factor in employee retention. People quit bosses, not jobs. And they stay for them, too.

3　You can create your employee Dream Team by hiring the right people for the right positions, and connecting your people with each other so that you are all acting as a cohesive whole.

4　Becoming a Mentor Manager creates stronger influence, increased profitability, and loyalty that lasts.

5　Your job as a Mentor Manager is to spark the possibilities in the people you lead.

6　People work at their best in a safe, encouraging, and calm environment. You can create this environment by keeping things simple.

7　When you give your employees a sense of ownership over their job and their career, they feel more invested in developing their skills—and in the company's success.

8　You must let people do their jobs, but check in continually to see how they're doing and to find out their status and what they need.

9　Hard times reveal true character—how you respond is what people will remember most.

10　Mentors *always* need mentoring.

11　And, finally, your employee's job is one part of a larger life, and that life requires passion, purpose, and the ability to provide.

Being a mentor and a leader is a role that should not be taken lightly. I can't think of another position that gives you as much opportunity to influence the lives of others for the better. You have the chance to create connections with your people in a way that will have a lasting and powerful effect on who they are and who they become. Think of Nancy the restaurant chain manager, who felt genuine, authentic care for her staff and who received that same love and loyalty in return. Think of Lee the Bell Captain, who held up a joyful mirror and let others see who they really are. Think of Mr. Jensen, who saw potential when everyone else saw a problem. Be a Nancy. Be a Lee. Be a Mr. Jensen. You'll be opening up the chance to do something greater than yourself, every single day.

The greatest part about your role in leadership is that it matters. The hardest part is that it matters every day. The best things in life are often brought about by small means consistently applied over time. Mentorship and leadership are no different. A Mentor Manager simply creates little, individual moments, day by day, that change the lives of those they lead and associate with, in big ways and small—creating an environment where the thought "I love it here" extends past the workplace and into the larger world.

My challenge to you, your final moment to master, is this: stand up for your responsibility to yourself, to your business, and to the people you lead, and become the type of leader that makes people say "I love it here." You have the tools and the ability to become this rare and influential mentor, and there is truly nothing in your way.

What an opportunity you have in front of you—to see "the kid who can't sit still" and to give them that metaphorical set of drumsticks. To watch them grow and flourish, not only in your business but in their larger lives as well. What a privilege and an honor to use your position to create relationships and foster personal development that will last a lifetime.

I've said it before and I will say it here, one last time: it's not about being the best *in* the world . . . it's about being the best *for* the world. If you can remember one thing from this book, I hope it's this.

ACKNOWLEDGMENTS

WRITING THIS book has been an exercise of perpetual anguish and turmoil, lasting years longer than I ever anticipated. It takes a lot, it turns out, to put your heart and research on paper in a coherent form, and I have deep gratitude for those people who helped push me beyond my perceived limits as an author. Through the years spent conducting research as the Undercover Millennial, through the endless writing and rewriting (and rewriting!), this has been a mountain that I never could have climbed on my own, and mere acknowledgment feels inadequate for the help and encouragement these individuals have offered during this process.

Some of my earliest readers include the incredible Robert Ferrell, Jess Fortier, Kevin Thomas, Lee Stoor, Rebecca Clark, Greg Trimble, Karen Harris, my wonderful mother Shauna Pulver, Brandon Simmons, Kelly Pulver, Steve Soelberg, and Dave Hennessey. All of these people gave gentle encouragement while steering me away from the remarkable mediocrity that made up my earliest drafts. I've had an incredible editorial and design team: Jesse Finkelstein, Caela Moffet, and Chris Brandt of Page Two, my publishing and marketing consultants who have consistently cared and guided my journey. Peter Cocking and Jaron Pulver were the inspirations behind the elegance, style, and design of the book, making it something I was passionate about not only for its content, but also for its look and feel.

Tiffany and Shawn Fletcher helped pick up my scattered pieces when I needed it most, and the insightful Catherine Oliver helped me to not repeat myself seventy-seven times on the same page and showed me enormous possibilities I hadn't seen before. The support of the brilliant Melissa Edwards and her incredible editing has turned my mess of words into a message that actually makes sense, elevating its impact and ability to connect with audiences at every level. My own "board of book mentors" saved me infinite amounts of time, money, and effort with their guidance as a young and clueless author with a dream. Thanks also goes to Phil Jones, Jason Hewlett, Scott Stratten, Ty Bennett, Michelle McCullough, Chad Hymas, Grant Baldwin, Michael Bungay Stanier, and Ian Altman for always believing in me and for creating moments of connection that made my message and this book stronger.

Someone once said that a man with strong dreams needs a woman with strong vision. Kelly Marie Pulver, you're my leading lady. Only God himself knows how much I couldn't have done this without you. You never stopped helping me climb this mountain with your endless amounts of support, sacrifice, time, guidance, and encouragement. I love you, always.

NOTES

Chapter 1: A Single Moment in Time

1 Michael Dimock, "Defining Generations: Where Millennials End and Generation Z Begins," Pew Research Center, January 17, 2019, pewresearch.org/fact-tank/2019/01/17/where-millennials-end-and-generation-z-begins.

2 Work Institute, *2020 Retention Report: Insights on 2019 Turnover Trends, Reasons, Costs & Recommendations*, info.workinstitute.com/en/retention-report-2020.

Chapter 2: Are You the Problem or the Solution?

1 Work Institute, *2020 Retention Report*.

2 Bill Conerly, "Companies Need to Know the Dollar Cost of Employee Turnover," *Forbes*, August 12, 2018, forbes.com/sites/billconerly/2018/08/12/companies-need-to-know-the-dollar-cost-of-employee-turnover.

3 David Allen, *Retaining Talent: A Guide to Analyzing and Managing Employee Turnover*, Society for Human Research Management Foundation, 2008, shrm.org/hr-today/trends-and-forecasting/special-reports-and-expert-views/documents/retaining-talent.pdf.

4 Work Institute, *2020 Retention Report*.

5 Tom Gimbel, "How to Help Millennials and Baby Boomers Get Along," *Fortune*, April 1, 2017, fortune.com/2017/04/01/leadership-career-advice-millennials-conflict-feud-mentorship.

6 Deloitte, *2018 Deloitte Millennial Survey: Millennials Disappointed in Business, Unprepared for Industry 4.0*, www2.deloitte.com/

content/dam/Deloitte/global/Documents/About-Deloitte/gx-2018-millennial-survey-report.pdf.

7   Society to Improve Diagnosis in Medicine, "Consensus Statement," January 27, 2020, improvediagnosis.org/consensusstatement.

8   As cited in Karlyn Borysenko, "How Much Are Your Disengaged Employees Costing You?" *Forbes*, May 2, 2019, forbes.com/sites/karlynborysenko/2019/05/02/how-much-are-your-disengaged-employees-costing-you.

Chapter 3: Creating Your Dream Team

1   CareerBuilder, "Nearly Three in Four Employers Affected by a Bad Hire, According to a Recent CareerBuilder Survey," December 7, 2017, press.careerbuilder.com/2017-12-07-nearly-three-in-four-employers-affected-by-a-bad-hire-according-to-a-recent-careerbuilder-survey.

2   As cited in J.T. O'Donnell, "85 Percent of Job Applicants Lie on Resumes. Here's How to Spot a Dishonest Candidate," *Inc.*, August 15, 2017, inc.com/jt-odonnell/staggering-85-of-job-applicants-lying-on-resumes-.html.

3   Freek Vermeulen, "Stop Comparing Management to Sports," *Harvard Business Review*, June 2, 2016, hbr.org/2016/06/stop-comparing-management-to-sports.

Chapter 4: The Mentor Manager

1   Tim S. Grover (@ATTACKATHLETICS), Twitter post, August 10, 2015, 7:09 a.m., twitter.com/ATTACKATHLETICS/status/630742880504692736.

2   As cited in Randall Beck and James Harter, "Why Good Managers Are So Rare," *Harvard Business Review*, March 13, 2014, hbr.org/2014/03/why-good-managers-are-so-rare.

3   Stephen R. Covey, *Primary Greatness: The 12 Levers of Success* (Simon & Schuster, 2015).

4   As cited in Sabrina Munns, "Employee Turnover Rates by Industry Comparison," e-days Absence Management, 2019, e-days.com/news/employee-turnover-rates-an-industry-comparison.

Chapter 6: Keep It Simple

1   Wayne Muller, *Sabbath: Finding Rest, Renewal, and Delight in Our Busy Lives* (Bantam, 1999).
2   The American Institute of Stress, "Workplace Stress," stress.org/ workplace-stress.
3   The American Institute of Stress, "What Is Stress?" stress.org/ daily-life.
4   Karen Allen, Barbara E. Shykoff, and Joseph L. Izzo Jr., "Pet Ownership, but Not ACE Inhibitor Therapy, Blunts Home Blood Pressure Responses to Mental Stress," *Hypertension* 2001(38), April 1, 2018, doi.org/10.1161/hyp.38.4.815.
5   Stephanie McMains and Sabine Kastner, "Interactions of Top-Down and Bottom-Up Mechanisms in Human Visual Cortex," *Journal of Neuroscience* 31(2), January 12, 2011, doi.org/ 10.1523/JNEUROSCI.3766-10.2011.
6   Mohamed Boubekri, Ivy N. Cheung, Kathryn J. Reid, Chia-Hui Wang, and Phyllis C. Zee, "Impact of Windows and Daylight Exposure on Overall Health and Sleep Quality of Office Workers: A Case-Control Pilot Study," *Journal of Clinical Sleep Medicine* 10(6), June 15, 2014, doi.org/10.5664/jcsm.3780.
7   C. Thøgersen-Ntoumani, E.A. Loughren, F.-E. Kinnafick, I.M. Taylor, J.L. Duda, and K.R. Fox, "Changes in Work Affect in Response to Lunchtime Walking in Previously Physically Inactive Employees: A Randomized Trial," *Scandinavian Journal of Medicine & Science in Sports* 25(6), January 6, 2015, doi.org/ 10.1111/sms.12398.
8   J.D. Lane, R.A. Adcock, R.B. Williams, and C.M. Kuhn, "Caffeine Effects on Cardiovascular and Neuroendocrine Responses to Acute Psychosocial Stress and Their Relationship to Level of Habitual Caffeine Consumption," *Psychosomatic Medicine* 52(3), May–June 1990, doi.org/10.1097/00006842-199005000-00006.

Chapter 9: Brace for Impact

1   Maria Cohut, "How Does Stress Affect the Brain?" *Medical News Today*, October 25, 2018, medicalnewstoday.com/ articles/323445.

Chapter 10: Your Personal Board of Mentors

1   Catherine Clifford, "Google Execs Reveal Secrets to Success They Got from Silicon Valley's 'Trillion Dollar' Business Coach," CNBC, April 17, 2019, cnbc.com/2019/04/17/google-execs-reveal-secrets-to-success-from-ceo-coach-bill-campbell.html.

2   Akin Ojumu, "Will Talent Out This Time?" *The Guardian*, March 24, 2002, theguardian.com/culture/2002/mar/24/awardsandprizes.film.

3   Zach Lowe, "Brad Stevens and the Celtics Have a Special Brand of Toughness," ESPN, May 11, 2018, espn.com/nba/story/_/id/23465885/zach-lowe-boston-celtics-toughness-nba-playoffs.

Chapter 11: Helping Them Live, Not Just Exist

1   Jim Clifton, "The World's Broken Workplace," Gallup Chairman's Blog, June 13, 2017, news.gallup.com/opinion/chairman/212045/world-broken-workplace.aspx.

2   Paul Taylor, Cary Funk, and Peyton Craighill, *Once Again, the Future Ain't What It Used to Be*, Pew Research Center, May 2, 2006, pewresearch.org/wp-content/uploads/sites/3/2010/10/betteroff.pdf.

Chapter 12: Small Things over a Long Period of Time

1   Kathleen McAuliffe, "The Undiscovered World of Thomas Edison," *The Atlantic*, December 1995, theatlantic.com/magazine/archive/1995/12/the-undiscovered-world-of-thomas-edison/305880.

2   B.C. Forbes, "Why Do So Many Men Never Amount to Anything?" *American Magazine* 91, January 1921.

CONTINUE THE CONVERSATION

Continue the conversation and connect personally with Clint:

Instagram: @clintpulver

Facebook: facebook.com/clint.pulver

YouTube: youtube.com/user/clintpulver

LinkedIn: linkedin.com/in/clintpulver

Twitter: @clintpulver

Website: clintpulver.com

PHOTO BY NATE EDWARDS

ABOUT
THE AUTHOR

CLINT PULVER is a professional keynote speaker, author, musician, pilot, and workforce expert. Known as the leading authority on employee retention, Clint has transformed how corporations like Keller Williams, AT&T, and Hewlett Packard create lasting loyalty through his work and research as the Undercover Millennial. He has been featured by *BusinessQ Magazine* as a "Top 40 Under 40," and, as a professional drummer, he has appeared in feature films and on *America's Got Talent*. In 2020, Clint won an Emmy Award for his short film *Be a Mr. Jensen*, which tells the story of how a single moment in time—and one particular mentor—can change the course of a life.

BRING *I LOVE IT HERE* TO YOUR ORGANIZATION

Keynote and Management Training

Invite Clint (live or virtual) to your next company meeting, retreat, conference, or event, and let him inspire your managers to become the leader everyone wishes they had. Clint will dig further into his research in a way that's tailored to the needs of your organization, helping your managers and leaders know exactly what to do to elevate your people and organization to the next level. To find out more, visit clintpulver.com.

Video Master Class: Management Made Simple

Delve deeper into the art of mentor management with Clint's exciting video course! In fifty-two entertaining and easy-to-watch weekly master classes, you'll learn step-by-step how to bring out the best in your staff—and in yourself as a leader. Using real-world lessons from his years of undercover research in companies large and small, Clint will share surprising strategies and exclusive challenges that will change the way you understand leadership. Week by week for a full year, you'll gain the tools to connect with your employees in a way that truly helps them engage with their work and discover their own most valuable skills. Soon, your company will have a team it can truly rely on, and your employees will be saying, "I love it here."

Share this series with your management team or with your entire organization, or simply watch it yourself and take your next step down the path toward becoming a leader who is remembered forever. Get started and receive your first video at clintpulver.com.

Listen on Audible

Don't just read it, experience it! *I Love It Here* is also available as an audiobook on Audible and other platforms.

Bulk Purchases

Want to give *I Love It Here* to your entire management team? Contact us at clintpulver.com/book to arrange a bulk order.

If you enjoyed this book and its message, please consider offering your review on Amazon, Goodreads, or your favorite online forum.